IRISHMAN DIES
from
STUBBORNNESS

Unbelievable
Truths Behind
the Life That
Launched the
Viral Obituary of
Christopher
Clifford Connors

CAITLIN CONNORS

HOUNDSTOOTH
PRESS

Irishman Dies from Stubbornness
Unbelievable Truths Behind the Life That Launched the Viral Obituary of Christopher Clifford Connors

FIRST EDITION

ISBN 978-1-5445-3873-0 Hardcover
978-1-5445-3874-7 Paperback
978-1-5445-3875-4 Ebook
978-1-5445-3995-9 Audiobook

Credit: Chapter illustrations created by the DALL-E 2 deep learning model developed by OpenAI.

For my brothers, Chris and Liam:

I can't bring Dad back, but I can tell you his stories.

For my baby boy, Caleb:

You have your grandfather's blue eyes.

Use responsibly.

IRISHMAN DIES

from

STUBBORNNESS

Did you find this book? Did it change you? Tell us your story. #irishmanfound

CONTENTS

"I might have been given a bad break,

but I've got an awful lot

to live for."

—LOU GEHRIG

AUTHOR'S NOTE

For those of you who wonder if we still get sad (the "we" who've lost someone suddenly, dramatically, or untimely), I'll try and answer for all of us.

We don't cry at movies when people die, even though we think we should. Contrived sad songs, old photos, or locations sometimes won't bring any tears, so you don't have to anxiously watch us like that.

It's at the strangest hour, when everyone has forgotten to worry about us, when we're deep in the mundane PowerPoint of living. It's on a 7:00 a.m. flight to a work meeting, when we're reading about diversity statistics in the *Harvard Business Review* and Boz Scaggs's "I Just Go" comes through our headset, and he *loved* Boz Scaggs. Suddenly it's happening—he's talking to us again, even though the lyrics aren't about death. And then we're sobbing in seat 13B on our way to a financial review 30,000 feet in the air.

And that's how it happens.

INTRODUCTION

I always wanted to write a book, but I never had a story. I didn't know how to come up with a plotline, and sometimes when I thought of one, I was frozen on the page because I didn't know how to make up an ending. Since I was only used to writing what I knew, and I didn't have an ending to my own life, how could I easily tie up whatever journey I wanted to take a reader on?

Then my dad died. That night, around a fire, his friends and family shared memories that inspired his obituary—one he had asked me to write for him in the final months we had together. We retold the time he hunted black bears in Russia and jumped out of the helicopter onto the cold tundra like an "Irish Popsicle for the bears," as he would say. And how so many people claimed he invented limo surfing in the '80s while working on Wall Street. The stories seemed endless, and we all smiled for the first time since he passed.

I posted the obituary to the local paper the next day, as is the journey of most death notices in small towns, with an ending sentence stating where his wake would be held (although we preferred calling it his "Celebration of Life"). Eight hours after it was posted, I received a text that BarStoolSports.com had shared his obituary using the headline "This Is Without A Doubt The Best Obituary I've Ever Read." Twelve hours after that, I received a call from *Inside Edition*. And just forty-eight hours after my dad had passed away, his Celebration of Life was crashed by strangers from around the world who came to pay homage via the bar tab to a man they said had changed their lives through his stories.

When a man's obituary goes viral, it means one of two things: his life was more interesting than any book or it resonated with the hearts of people worldwide. In the case of Christopher Clifford Connors, it was both.

I realized I'd found the story I wanted to tell.

On the heels of this post-mortem connection that Dad had with people everywhere, I decided to keep writing. I bought a cheap tape recorder, wrote down the names of all the people who were with him through the biggest phases of his life, and then headed out to interview them all. The trail that this obituary made kept my dad alive and made a traditionally sad moment into something larger than any of us.

When everything settled down and the emails stopped coming in ("The obituary is on the front page of a New Zealand news-paper!" "I was just listening to the radio, and they dedicated a song to Chris Connors!"), I started to transcribe the interviews. Interviewing Dad's friends over beers and meats had been a way to stay close to him, but once I sat down to write, I had to admit that I still had no plot and, worse than that, no plan.

While mindlessly transcribing what others had lived, I started writing what I had lived. It was the easiest place for me to start because all I had to do was write what I saw the day my dad had died. That chapter, which was an expansion of the first line of the obituary, became the first chapter of the book you now hold in your hands.

That chapter also eventually led to five more from my point of view as Chris Connors's daughter, written from the heart about how I saw him and how I thought he saw me. I didn't know if the rambunctious audience who read the obituary would have any interest in the increasing seriousness of my chapters, so I intercut my chapters with Dad's headliner moments (e.g., training with Navy SEALs, being a Golden Gloves boxer, becoming a legend on Wall Street), retold by those who were there with him. This gave the book a balance of lightness and heaviness but also provided a balanced view of who he was.

While we all thought we knew who Christopher Clifford Connors was, it wasn't until I compiled and printed his stories together in this book that I could see him as he was completely. It was like various sides of a prism coming together, all of us telling a different side to his story, a side only we could see.

All was well and good until I had to edit the interviews. Those sections (more like trains of thought without guardrails) sat looking at me for months. I tried to edit them (some people spoke more eloquently than others; some jumped around; some had no story at all); but I eventually found myself in the quicksand of not knowing how to bring a reader into a story I wasn't there to experience. I wasn't there to experience the smells and sounds of the ocean, so how could I write about a sailboat sinking? I didn't want my sentences to come off as simple and pedestrian, but I also couldn't take to the literary floor and dance the English language into detail the way that came easily to me when it was my own point of view.

The book sat for five years that way. All because I couldn't figure out how to write the interviews (and probably also because I didn't want to let a world of strangers, family, and friends down by telling his stories badly and doing my dad a disservice; a man who wasn't here to approve of the manuscript).

I got married. I had a baby. Then I needed a new challenge; so one night in 2022, I opened a bottle of Sassicaia and double-clicked that old Word document on my desktop. Far enough removed that I no longer felt the need to achieve perfection, I started reading and rewriting the interviews. I let the stories tell themselves without my overthinking getting in the way, making the headway that only someone who wants to move on can.

As for my chapters, my experiences of being Chris Connors's daughter, they became the ones I ended up being scared of publishing. Writing a book is a revealing and humbling experience.

It's the equivalent of giving you keys to my house for a week to open any drawer you please, especially the underwear drawer. I can fake a story, and I've faked many great things, but it's distressing to write and share what I have felt in its rawness because that means giving up control of what I want you to feel. I became like a director coming out to stand in front of the camera with no script.

Don't get me wrong: I want people to read this book, of course. I am sharing these stories despite my insecurities because Dad's story needs to be shared; any one side of this refracted lens could reflect in you something you need to see. But selfishly I also don't want to know that you've read this book because that means you've seen through the cinematography and have seen me for who I am and was. So if I'm ever at dinner or having a drink with you, don't tell me you've read this. Because then I'll know you've looked through my underwear drawer, and we may both feel uncomfortable.[1]

---

[1] Lawyer's note: We have removed the last names of all supporting characters to protect anonymity (and because we also forgot some of them).

┌───┐

Reprint of the original obituary
"Irishman Dies from Stubbornness, Whiskey"
by Caitlin Connors

└───┘

C hris Connors died, at age 67, after trying to box his bikini-clad hospice nurse just moments earlier. Ladies man, game slayer, and outlaw Connors told his last inappropriate joke on Friday, December 9, 2016, that which cannot be printed here. Anyone else fighting ALS and stage 4 pancreatic cancer would have gone quietly into the night, but Connors was stark naked drinking Veuve in a house full of friends and family as Al Green played from the speakers. The way he died is just like he lived: he wrote his own rules, he fought authority and he paved his own way. And if you said he couldn't do it, he would make sure he could.

Most people thought he was crazy for swimming in the ocean in January; for being a skinny Irish Golden Gloves boxer from Quincy, Massachusetts; for dressing up as a priest and then proceeding to get into a fight at a Jewish deli. Many gawked at his start of a career on Wall Street without a financial background — but instead with an intelligent, impish smile, love for the spoken word, irreverent sense of humor, and stunning blue eyes that could make anyone fall in love with him.

As much as people knew hanging out with him would end in a night in jail or a killer screwdriver hangover, he was the type of man that people would drive 16 hours at the drop of a dime to come see. He lived 1000 years in the 67 calendar years we had with him because he attacked life; he grabbed it by the lapels, kissed it, and swung it back onto the dance floor. At the age of 26 he planned to circumnavigate the world—instead, he ended up spending 40 hours on a life raft off the coast of Panama. In 1974, he founded the Quincy Rugby Club. In his thirties, he sustained a knife wound after saving a woman from being mugged in New York City. He didn't slow down: at age 64, he climbed to the base camp of Mount Everest. Throughout his life, he was an accomplished hunter and birth control device tester (with some failures, notably Caitlin Connors, 33; Chris Connors, 11; and Liam Connors, 8).

He was a rare combination of someone who had a love of life and a firm understanding of what was important—the simplicity of living a life with those you love. Although he threw some of the most memorable parties during the greater half of a century, he would trade it all for a night in front of the fire with his family in Maine. His acute awareness of the importance of a life lived with the ones you love over any material possession was only handicapped by his territorial attachment to the remote control of his Sonos music.

Chris enjoyed cross dressing, a well-made fire, and mashed potatoes with lots of butter. His regrets were few, but include eating a rotisserie hot dog from an unmemorable convenience store in the summer of 1986.

Of all the people he touched, both willing and unwilling, his most proud achievement in life was marrying his wife Emily Ayer Connors who supported him in all his glory during his heyday, and lovingly supported him physically during their last days together.

Absolut vodka and Simply Orange companies are devastated by the loss of Connors. A "Celebration of Life" will be held during Happy Hour (4 p.m.) at York Harbor Inn on Monday, December 19.

In lieu of flowers, please pay open bar tab or donate to Connors' water safety fund at www.thechrisconnorsfund.com.

Chapter 1

"I'M NOT DEAD YET"

December 2016. York, Maine

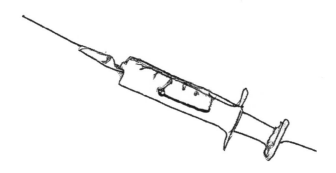

It takes a man with cowboy grit to be standing where others have succumbed, near a soft bed and the nurturing hands of hospice nurses who were ready to ease the pain with drugs that in any other situation could have been exciting.

Chris Connors wasn't a cowboy, but he did market himself to those who knew him as a young Paul Newman. Once a Golden Glove boxer, he was now fighting for his life in what was turning out to be his last bout in the ring, a first-floor guest room in his home in York, Maine, on Rams Head Lane. He didn't know how to win this one, but he thought remaining standing upright would be a good start.

The muscles that were atrophying within his throat and in the Union Valley of both hands (the area acupuncturists call *He Gu* or 合谷, that thumb meat we press sometimes when we have headaches) were accustomed to giving 120 percent at the eleventh hour: once when he was seventeen in a sweat-stained boxing ring at the old Boston Arena, trying to sustain a broken nose during an eleven-round stretch; once at age forty-five experiencing Heartbreak Hill for the first time during the Boston Marathon race that he had in no way qualified for; once at age fifty-nine mountain biking in Moab, Utah; once at age sixty-two doing one-armed pushups in the mud with twenty-year-old Navy SEALs; and now at age sixty-seven when the world seemed to be wondering why a man in comfort care, days from passing away, was dancing an Irish jig next to his bed. He was trying to ward off death with a dose of crazy just enough to stop people from asking anymore questions.

Unfortunately (or fortunately), standing next to my dad at this exact moment were two people even crazier than he was: retired Navy SEALs whose cheeks, if you looked closely, still had night-vision goggle indents from a mission the week prior (although this cannot be fact-checked by this publishing company). Both men had dropped issues of national security (or, at the least, serious paperwork) without thinking twice when they got the call from my dad, someone with whom they had survived many arduous and impossible adventures. Now their old friend was asking them to do what would be hard for many men: watch a once-mighty fighter lose a fight, help hold him up and help lay him down during his last days.

They stood on each side of Dad now, trying to steady his freckled legs as he fought against them. Instead of Rothco tactical vests and pixelated Type II uniforms, they wore cotton drawstring pants. They had traded in their starch-white Jiu Jitsu gis and sniper crosshairs to be here at this moment, aiming a needle full of Lorazepam at a new type of target: Chris's remaining ass fat. (The Lorazepam was prescribed to calm anxiety and help any labored breathing.) They found themselves wielding a weapon with an unknown circular error probable.

"We're the good guys, Chris," said one SEAL, giving his best marketing pitch to his wriggling best friend who hated the whole ridiculous inconvenience of dying. Dad was moving to elude this needle as if it were death itself.

The other SEAL had an idea. Dad's many accomplishments were fueled by a lifelong OCD and anxiety that, when mixed, were enough to energize the body in times of emergencies and cripple any laziness during times the body should have been at rest. This fight-or-flight was an opportunity for the man holding the needle that sedated Dad enough to lay him down. Perhaps he could get Dad to back into the needle during one of these fitful premortem adrenaline spikes, a soul's last argument to the jury.

Dad struggled in the SEALs' arms and did in fact yank himself right towards the four-inches of needle locked on his unsuspecting butt muscle. It was at this exact moment that my dad's brain circuits relayed the new information of what had happened to his posterior all the way to his amygdala. This sent an impulse to his autonomic nervous system, resulting in a sort of Big Bang, an explosion of flight energy. Dad immediately donkey-kicked the needle-holding SEAL with enough force to throw the syringe across the room.

The syringe landed in front of the hospice nurse that York Hospital had sent over to help keep this circus at bay. She was stunned, as any mentally balanced individual would be. Her patience for the Connors's way of courting death had run as thin as the watered-down, overly vodka-infused orange juice in a dewing Tervis tumbler, forgotten long ago on a cedar bookshelf somewhere in the house—a beverage manifestation of one of Dad's many final attempts to maintain normalcy.

The motor memory of pouring a screwdriver (which his throat muscles refused to let him drink) was as calming for him as his showers, both activities more frequent than eating. Dad had decided he wasn't ready to lie down and die just yet and maybe a drink would make things better. This also went hand in hand with a spike in his confidence to take on the day as he had done in healthier times. During these specific instances when Dad thought he was ready to take on a new project, he went into his office and started making phone calls, like the call we found out he made to his landscapers only when they arrived the next day and started unloading thousands of dollars of rocks onto our lawn. Because of this, the sound of an ice cube dispenser or a distant shower elicited anxiety in his wife, Emily, for what mission he was about to incite.

Many important decisions were made by my dad in those last few weeks, unbeknownst to Emily, decisions which came to fruition weeks later in the form of massive bills that surprised Dad himself who, at that point, had forgotten he'd made any calls. If Emily was lucky, sometimes Dad's special project was as simple as cleaning his antique gun collection in the basement (although another surprise came almost a year after his death, when she opened a DHL box stamped from Italy only to discover a pair of antique blunderbusses, Dad's final bid and winning item from his favorite online auction house). Even in the last few weeks of his life he still walked to the backyard to shoot some of the guns he had spent so many years amassing. For the neighbors, the gunshots were a welcome break from his bow-and-arrow sessions, periods of time when they could anticipate whizzing weapons impaling their yellowing fall lawn, always too close to some nearby dog.

Emily and I didn't know those were his last weeks. We begged the doctor for a timeline we could stand on, if only to help us wrap our minds around how much longer we had to deal with the responsibility of our feelings and the feelings of others. "How are you holding up?" they'd ask, with a skittish face and heavy pause that was ripe with hope. We spared them the reality of the situation and instead opted for an answer that was palatable enough for them to continue their day.

We also wanted to know how much longer we had to watch as the once-alive house, which always had bedrooms strewn with summer luggage from visiting friends, suddenly made people nervous to enter. How much longer until we could relax in our ignorance again and get back to taking each other for granted? Ungratefulness was a comforting pastime; finding annoyance in the unimportant, like the innocuous sounds of a healthy human who brushed their teeth too loudly, meant that life was okay.

The quietness that filled the home now seemed uncharacteristic of its past receptions, but the home always served as a beautiful backdrop to all our milestone moments. Most of the expansive house on the river was decorated with heavy wooden queen- and king-sized beds, mahogany furniture, sensibly patterned wallpaper, and gilded frames holding a variety of oil paintings. Each room had some framed variation of ships at a feisty sea, their billowing sails either alight with a soft yellow sun or grayed by a cloudy sky, scenes that looked as if they'd been steeped in tea and removed just in time to make everything seem as dreary as old butterscotch. The only variety in the artwork was that some of these warships and whaleboats were lucky enough to have been painted with the safety of nearby land in the background, sepia horizons with stern, white church steeples and buildings with brown parallelogram roofs casting precise shadows on a seventeenth-century Portsmouth afternoon. Most of the paintings in the house held just one lonely boat (Cutty Sarks were his favorite), never a fleet, and the boats were either in the middle of some storm at sea or floating alone in the channel, surrounded only by tiny fishing vessels if they had any company at all.

Because stairs were a problem for the pain of cancer and the wane of ALS, Dad eventually had to move into the downstairs guest bedroom. We used to enter the area Dad was now fighting for his life in only to change the sheets for new holiday guests or grab a light bulb from the wooden console along the east wall.

The space had three large windows that let in the sleepy afternoon sun; the dusted sunlight was the only thing to fill the air of the usually empty room. Now that Dad was staying here the air smelled like his soap and mint toothpaste—clean, despite being alive with expiration. Bleached-white hand towels lay flat on top of his wooden nightstand and dresser, Dad's wares neatly lined and spaced onto the fresh cotton like the spread of a surgeon's leather rollup. Instead of various types of physician's obstetrics and bistouries (folding knives and lancets with tortoiseshell handles), there were toiletries and small scissors from his leather patina Dopp bag (the same set of small scissors that Emily and I tried to steal from Dad last week, having recently caught him sitting on the edge of his bed after lunch, his empty belly folded in as he tried to remove the morphine pump attached to him).

Today, December 8, 2016, the bottom panes of those eastern windows were shuttered against the kind of soft afternoon light that eludes all beginner painters. The room was packed with more people than it's ever had, the majority of us watching Chris Connors grapple with a losing battle. It was that moribund environment most visitors avoided, fearing the air my dad was having trouble breathing would suffocate them as well. Dad could always draw a crowd, and today seemed no different. His Navy SEAL friends, the hospice nurse, the unfortunate tagalong nurse trainee, his wife, daughter, youngest brother Russell, Russell's wife and daughter Liz, and a curious golden retriever puppy (who was now larger than Dad) were now in the middle of a scene unfolding in a way that no one could have predicted.

Moments before Dad's anti-Lorazepam outburst I had been busy trying to keep myself afloat above the heavy air of imminence rising all around us. We were all trying to ignore the insidious conclusions cresting over our heads and casting shadows that we couldn't quite see. I tried to bring the breathable oxygen of normalcy back to the room by talking too much, something I tended to do in tense situations. Every time I did this, though, my thoughts seemed to get trapped inside a balloon that floated farther and farther away from me until I had completely forgotten why I had started talking at all.

This whole crowded scene was lit only by one lamp, giving it the lighting of a baby's room during afternoon nap time (which wasn't too far from the current situation, barring the age of the napper). We had been taking care of him like a newborn, but Dad had refused to be an invalid, both verbally (during the previous year) and via his moxie (this year). Actually, he had specifically asked not to be in this living state, a purgatory of existence sustained by someone else's hands, an understandable living hell for someone who had been the captain his whole life. In fact, except for the few formative years in the early 1950s when he hadn't yet learned to walk, he was in control.

Dad had his shot of benzodiazepines and was now walking just as determinedly as when he first tried out his chubby baby legs. He should have been unsteady, sleepy even, but he was wobbling forward on two legs lined with a shadow of muscle, one calf softened with a now-healed scar from being stabbed intervening in a New York City mugging. Unlike the fanfare and encouragement that his life's first steps were met with however, everyone around him now was trying to get him to lie down. Instead of celebrating him for walking, Emily held his tiny freckled arm and pleaded he relax just for a bit.

The rest of the brigade looked at each other, astonished that a body pumped full of more pain medication than a retired Saratoga thoroughbred was still refusing to give in. It made it even more amazing that, just a few weeks ago, Dad had mustered enough willpower to tighten his depleted throat muscles and speak succinctly, a special occasion he reserved not for moments of enlightenment or goodbyes but instead for a joke.

"I'm not dead yet," he had said with an English accent, quoting a *Monty Python* skit he thought was hysterical and apparently tactful in his current situation. In his state, he didn't know his way out of a room with four doors, but he could sense that the sitting party of visiting guests around him were expecting that very ending, as if death were a train scheduled to arrive. While the jobs and relationships that waited for the rest of us continued to pedal forward in a world of interlocking time and date gears,

Chris's final audience wore the politeness required of the waiting bereaved, stuck in time in a motionless moment, the occasional cross-legged foot tremors giving away to their thinning composure. Dad, despite all the projected ignorance we put on patients who can't speak to us anymore, had called their bluff. With that one Monty Python line, he reminded everyone in the room that he was still at the helm and death could take a number.

Now I suspect Dad could feel the room was heavy with the air that I had failed to talk into lightness; he could sense the storm approaching before his loyal crew could track it in their sight. At that moment, held up by his wife and surrounded by a group of his favorite people whose faces looked to him of nervous soldiers handling a dusty IED, he gave his final attempt at lightening the mood. And so, with his throat too weakened by ALS to crack a full joke, he lifted his spotted chicken legs (an epithet penned by his high school football coach) and stepdanced more spritely than anything Michael Flatley could have asked for. His feet sprung from the clean carpet, crossing ankle over ankle, one silent beat at a time. We stood in wonderment. Dad was doing a bedside jig eighteen hours and thirty-two minutes before he died, succeeding in lifting the heaviness of the room (as Irishmen often do) one last time.

The hospice nurse, whose back was against the wall in a dimly lit corner, could count on one hand the number of people she'd seen die standing up. It seemed Chris was going to be one of them.

1960s:
SPIDER SPOT
CONNORS

Created from the memories of
Ed Vena and Bob Bertoli,
Chris's oldest friends.

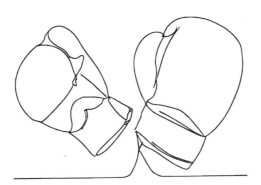

In the mid-60s, all Chris seemed to think about was girls and athletics—he was very accomplished in one of those pursuits, not so much the other. Since he was not the best athlete, he had to play to his strengths when picking a sport. He was a skinny, teenaged Irish kid from Quincy who had no plans but to be ready to fight each day that arose from the night.

His friends were, for the most part, more skilled than Chris but no one had more desire to succeed than him. He tried track and football (any sport where bullheadedness could gain points always suited him well), but mostly always was coming close to being thrown off the teams for various indiscretions and pugnacity. As cocaptains of the football team, we were always intervening with the coach to keep him because he had courage, and that isn't something that could be taught.

Luckily for Chris, courage was the only thing required of anyone to get into boxing.

At North Quincy High, there was a boy a year or so ahead of us who participated in a Golden Glove competition, which created a lot of buzz at the school. The notoriety generated from the competition resonated with Chris enough that he decided to enter in the Massachusetts Golden Glove competition the following year.

By 1966 Chris was boxing at the old Boston Arena, now Northeastern University's hockey rink. If you look up this fact, you won't find it, not even in the *Patriot Ledger*; he boxed there under the *nom de guerre* of "Spider Spots Connors" as a lightweight. "Spots" was an endearing nickname for anyone with that amount of freckles.

To prepare for the fight, Chris chose Bob and another friend, Bill, to be his cornermen. There was not two ounces of boxing knowledge among the three of them, but what they did have was all the time in the world: 365 days to train a man who didn't know how to take a hit in the ring. They sent Chris jogging down Wollaston Beach, confident that he already knew how to brace for impact. (They weren't wrong; this is a guy who, later in 1972, donned a football helmet and purposely totaled his car for the insurance money.)

We don't remember anything we told Chris in terms of technique, but we can distinctly remember those dark, filthy locker rooms where we prepared for his fight. We weren't the ones headed into the ring to fight, but we were scared to death in that room, terrified by the sounds and the smells of the other fighters who were all crowded in a tiny space waiting to be called into the arena.

We taped Chris's hands (again not knowing what we were doing), got him dressed, and gave him a small pep talk. He was speechless; maybe he was as scared as us, but he never told us. He was determined to fight. He wanted to be recognized as having the courage to go up against an unknown opponent in the Golden Gloves world, and he would not be backing out.

"Christopher Clifford Connors." When his name was finally called over the loudspeaker, we all got up and walked past the rest of the fighters in the locker room.

As we walked Chris to the ring, down an aisle with shouting crowds on both sides, we were both amazed and impressed by his bravery as he approached his opponent. Staring Chris down from above him in the ring was a Hispanic guy from Lawrence, Massachusetts, who was covered in tattoos that went far beyond the boundaries of his satin boxing trunks and striped boxing boots (two items that Chris could never afford). Before the round was clanged to start, Chris hopped around his corner, taking jabs at the air, sinew tightening within him. The springs underneath his feet responded with each landing. His boxing shoes were worn, with no special (expensive) outsoles to grip the mat for lightning-quick footwork. His snazzy opponent stood watching him from the opposite corner, making all kinds of menacing gestures at Chris as the crowd egged on the bloodbath. It looked like a bleak future for this bout.

When the bell rang, Chris went straight towards this guy's face and beat him up like we had never seen. His opponent took a knee before the second round.

Soon there were more and more fights for Chris, and more and more attention. After each fight, Chris was paid four dollars to compensate for any injuries he might get from fighting, but that cut money never went too far. High on the thrill of competition, we followed Chris, his dots of dark red blood trapped under oily Vaseline smears, to the Neponset package store to buy beer, where four dollars got us a cold case of sixteen-ounce Pabst Blue Ribbon longnecks.

After one particularly ego-boosting fighting year for Chris, when the drinking age at the time was sixteen, our goal was to hit as many bars as we could without getting carded. In Southie, there is a bar on every corner and most weren't carding. A swinging neon sign on one particular corner got the attention of Chris, who was more than a little over the blood-alcohol limit. He sauntered in and announced that he was the famous boxer "Spider Spots Connors," challenging anyone in there to a fight. If he had waited a few moments before his summons to contest, he would have seen that the bar he walked into was full of local, blue-collar workers whose hands were familiar with hard work. It was not one of his better decisions.

Besides those few midnight losses, when Monday mornings rolled around, our high school principal made announcements over the school-wide PA system about Chris's boxing match wins. Chris was proud of achieving this local fame and ready to use it to get some girls.

As Spider Spots Connors's popularity grew, so did his cut money—eventually costing him his amateur fighting status. Back then, being paid as a professional athlete disqualified you from amateur athletics, including the Golden Gloves fights and high school football.

Still, for the rest of his life, Chris was proud to be a former Golden Glove Champion. In fact, several years later when he was starting his financial career, he began participating in charity fights for his company. Quincy locals proudly knew him around town as "the Golden Gloves guy who fought in the Wall Street fights." The expungement of salty sweat reminded him of freedom beyond the paper chase—that under his suit, he was an untamable beast.

The people he met boxing and the reputation he made for himself in the sport began a chain of events that made up the rest of the decades beyond our high school years. You know, his life could probably fill a book if someone had the time to figure out the main players who hold all his stories, if they can even remember the details. Actually, it's probably near impossible to track down all the characters who would need to be interviewed anyway.

[Ed Vena is a retired lawyer living in Duxbury, Massachusetts, and Bob Bertoli is now retired and lives in Ridgewood, New Jersey.]

1970s–1980s:
THE DEFINITION
OF A GOOD MAN IS
COMPLICATED

Created from the memories of Russell Connors,

recounted over bourbon Manhattans in

his home in Kittery Point, Maine.

Various chapters of my life involved my older brother Chris, but he took different roles depending on the year. My memories start with him watching out for me, the youngest of six. Chris stood out from the rest of the Irish Catholic gaggle of children as he always seemed to be looking out for me when I was younger: the first child, Kevin, was too old to notice me; my existence was a torture on the middle child, Dougy; and my other brother, Billy, was always buried in a book. It was these four Connors brothers combined who had to be a challenge for my only sister, Sheila. But Chris had a soft spot for me, which felt really good as a little kid, especially as one whose chubby baby legs once ended up as a literal pin cushion, the result of my other brothers "firing" sewing needles into me from the hands of little green army men as I cried, stumbling on their LEGO buildings towards any escape. They called the game Godzilla.

When I was a teenager, Chris decided I was now worthy of a conversation. Years before he took a job on Wall Street, he was still deciding what to do with his life. Around this time he found himself doing fundraising for Ted Kennedy and running some political campaigns for Joe Kennedy, who happened to play rugby with Chris in Quincy, Massachusetts. He involved me in the campaigns he was running for the Kennedys, titling me Ward Captain. When I asked him what I was going to do as the Ward Captain, he simply replied, "Whatever I tell you to do." And that is exactly what I did, through both the good and bad action plans. When he told me to paste Kennedy signs all over his Cadillac, I didn't ask questions. When he told me later that day to jump in the car, I did. It wasn't until I saw the circles on a map in the front seat that I knew what was happening; we were swinging by all the local senior homes, where we'd tell any blue hair we saw that we would drive them to vote if they wanted a ride.

Working for him during the day began to pay off as he started to include me in his nights. In those years, my father kept a forty-foot boat on the Cape. Since my parents weren't around during the week, Chris took full advantage (or in sales what they call "seizing an opportunity") of those weeknights. He was the master of campaigning so there were lots of girls and there were a lot of parties.

When the boat was unavailable, the car would do for nighttime mischief. Imagine being seventeen years old, driving a little shitbox car, with your older brother in the back seat with a bunch of really pretty girls who you, the designated driver, aren't even going to get to look at too long in that rearview mirror. But for that moment in time, you're with them, one of them. You're breathing the same night air as they are and they're telling you about the music and they're singing, the whole car alive with the smell of Old Spice and East Coast breeze.

Sometimes they'd sneak me into the bars they were going to, giving me a momentary feeling of acceptance. I stood no chance with those girls, especially not with Chris Connors around. But I was coming of age, and he was bringing me along for the ride.

It was our oldest brother Kevin who offered Chris his first job on Wall Street, which was ironic because they always had a love-hate relationship that set the backdrop for a life of competition that ended without a winner. As the two oldest boys, Chris and Kevin were always trying to beat out the other one. Worse than that, Chris saw things through his own lens and Kevin through his, and neither view ever seemed to align. When Kevin got Chris a job in the financial world, the competition continued on their Bloombergs and off. When Chris was building his pool at his home in Red Bank, New Jersey, he went to Kevin's house just to measure

his pool so he could build his one foot longer. Their determination propelled both to fortune, lives anyone would covet,
but Chris was always looking beyond the present to something larger.

I have to tell you something important about what
happened between Chris and Kevin. This is hard,
because the definition of a good man is complicated.

I know all the contradictions when kids lie it's easier because there's
Kool-Aid all over their hands, even though they look right at
you and say, "I didn't spill that." you're being a prick
there wasn't a body
if you need some money, call Amex the Hainan
Island midair collision between a United States Navy signals

intelligence aircraft and a People's Liberation Army Navy interceptor fighter jet that resulted in an international dispute between the United States of America and the People's Republic of China. The US had to apologize. ██ ████ ██████████████ . ███ ██ ██████ ████ ███ ███ ████████████████████ They started emailing each other again, which mostly consisted of inappropriate jokes, and then one week later was 9/11.

██████████████ ████████████

██ ███ ██ █ Don't put any of this in your book.

Chris took very well to sales, and was soon hitting a stride on Wall Street. That stride meant that his first wife, Paula, got the raw end of the deal, as is the case with those closest to the fire. As destructive as the financial business was to the men and women who gave their lives to keeping it alive, many of those same bond salesmen and traders were destructive to the fragile things around them—and Chris liked to be more than irreverent in the '80s.

Paula was nine months pregnant when Chris took a shotgun to their backyard birdbath in the quiet suburbs of Shrewsbury, New Jersey, on a Sunday afternoon. Chris and his cohorts were laughing, reeling off a day of shooting skeet, when Paula came down the stairs and landed her fist on Chris's chin, knocking him down to the floor. He got up laughing, surprised and excited to tell everyone the next day at work.

Paula had the patience of an angel and she loved Chris but there's always a limit. Sometimes he got home from work at 3:00 a.m., a company car having picked him up from the office, carted him around various client dinners and other stop offs, and eventually drove him home to New Jersey. Chris had his limo driver come in and sleep on the couch for a few hours until they had to leave for work again in a few hours. Paula seemed to be flotsam in the new wakes Chris was making in the Big Apple, but he inevitably came walking in their front door with those big blue eyes and that Massachusetts accent. "Hi Paula," he would always say.

The irony was Chris's own mom had sealed herself a similar fate with her blue-eyed Irish husband; both women had to play the adult role when it came to running a house because of the men they had fallen in love with. If my dad on occasion typically was a bit too generous with his money, it left his wife to figure out how she'd be able to pay the bills for the rest of the month.

People always see the fun Irishman buying drinks at the bar and their grounded wives as the boring police, always pulling over the man for drinking too much (or, in Paula's case, punching him square in the nose to the applause of his friends). But God bless the police for hiding money under the mattress to pay the bills and keeping flying bullets out of suburban backyards.

Maybe all our wives chose a hard path when they married Connors men, my own wife included. I was campaigning with Chris even when we were older and both working in Manhattan. I remember calling home one night after work, telling my wife, "I'm running late," and hearing the click of her hanging up the phone because, in fact, I was already beyond the definition of late. I went to lunch on a Friday with him and three days later we'd be in a different city buying new clothes at whatever store was open.

The color of the Connors' light was bright, but anyone who ever was (or is) a "Connors-aholic" knows that these big crazy stories always come with a price. The most important thing I learned from running with the bulls is that you have to hang on to each other through it all. "Each other" is the only real thing we have.

[Russ Connors lives with his wife, Mary, on the southern coast of Maine where they enjoy that same quality of life that eventually drew his brother Chris to retire there.]

Chapter 2

ROLL CREDITS

1983–2016. York, Maine

I don't think he was ready to have me, an offspring and especially a girl. Having to talk to his nine-year-old daughter seemed to be as frustrating to him as making conversation with the ticket takers at the movie theater who didn't understand what my dad meant when he called a movie "black comedy" and thought he was just a racist middle-aged man.

Dad was in his early forties when I took my first breath. We didn't live together for long from what I understand, and by the time my brain decided to keep a space for memories he was working in Manhattan and sending my mom child support. His life was work and his life was New York City, but both seemed to be dragging him down because I never saw him smile much when he picked me up for our weekends together.

As a child of divorce I was allocated two weekends a month with Dad and a healthy portion of anxious attachments in my future relationships. Every other weekend he picked me up on his way down to the Jersey Shore from the city, knocking on my mom's apartment door in his work suit to say simply, "Hi Paula." We drove down to his beach house in Lavallette, New Jersey, mostly in silence because, despite my best efforts, I never could bring him out of his head. For a long time, I took his unhappiness as something I could strive to fix with humor or maybe by impressing him with my smarts. Neither of us could predict that in ten or so years he would remarry and have the son he felt it easier to bond with. And because he would be less stressed, he became a softer, more fun type of Dad. But in my childhood it was still just me and him. And despite not knowing what to say to each other, we were dedicated to teaming up every other weekend at that beach house, regardless of the season.

Lavallette's beaches bloomed with families and color during the warm summers; striped fabrics pulled across rusty beach chairs dotted the sand and the wind carried the screams from kids running in the still-cold water to cool down from the heat. In contrast, the winter seasons' bright gray sky and unfocused cloudy sun stung our eyes with all their silver qualities and kept us mostly indoors. We'd look out of the salt-fogged sliding glass doors on his waterfront first-floor rental to an empty shoreline and board-walk, beyond which the bitter cold wind pushed the waves back to reveal their white tips, shrapnel spraying the air. We were loyal to the beach house no matter the month, and were some of the few who kept the beds warm year round.

To keep myself busy when I saw Dad was lost in thought, I did things like climb the cabanas on the boardwalk at night to stare at the sky. I liked the sky in Lavallette because I could see every visible planet in their sea of stars, Jupiter and Mercury both clear from my earth. I lifted up my hand to try and cover some parts of the universe, then closed one eye and watched Mercury disappear beyond my thumb. I blinked the other eye, and I lost Jupiter; you can only see the full picture of things if you keep both eyes open.

Signing a year-long lease was an easy decision for Dad to make because those weekends in Lavallette were what he lived for, holding his breath in the smog of New York City and the lesser-known travel and entertainment expenses of time, sleep, and health. It seemed like the first breath of salt air brought him back to life. Back on 55th Street and Lexington Avenue, his studio apartment with galley kitchen was merely a place for him to eat takeout Moo Shu Pork or a tin-atomized Beefaroni, sleep for a couple of predawn hours, and hang the silk nooses he wore on weekdays at the office. In the city he was often attending to clients and his own id so thoroughly that he never even made it home to put a hand on his bed. Instead of a briefcase of papers, he brought to work one packed with a dress shirt and tie—his clothes for the next day. But here on New Jersey Avenue in Lavallette, where he could always hear the heartbeat of the ocean outside his window, here he could come up for air.

Saturday mornings he woke up hours before his teenage daughter in order to run five miles. While Dad was known to ski in Levi jeans, what was even more indicative of his New Jersey residency was the outfit he wore for these morning boardwalk runs: thick, gray sweatpants with unattractive early 90s elastic ankles and a logo-less gray sweatshirt, the hood of which was always draped over his head like a Rocky Balboa training run. Every morning, any season, and without fail, Dad donned his cotton tuxedo and ran up and down the splintery boardwalk until the full-body greenhouse he created allowed him to sweat out whatever toxins he had accumulated over the week: wine, steaks, strange skin, and familiar highs. I saw him return from these weekend runs with darkened gray sweat stains around the neck and arms of that thick fabric; it was enough to thoroughly disgust me and further my retreat into a hormonal girl's imagined solitude and elitism.

Some weekends I'd be miffed to find him bringing along a new girlfriend to our beach house. That meant both Saturday and Sunday I got to watch the new girl's song and dance, the one where they try to befriend the daughter as a way to get to the heart of the father. It was hard for them to get close to me though, because I was too young to need to impress anyone (my ego was not yet bruised), which is what they were expecting from their interactions with me. Unfortunately for them, all I had was my sense of whether I enjoyed someone's company, so I never warmed up to any of them. Dad always brought *me* back to the beach house, though, and I was always his movie date, and those gestures made me feel special.

Moviegoing knew no best season or time of day for us. We continued to see matinees together until Dad's last week alive, and I felt the same every time: privileged that he still asked me to accompany him. Sometimes in the winter months at the beach

Dad took me to the movies on Saturday and on Sunday too. Even though we didn't talk very much, we spent a lot of time together sitting shoulder to shoulder in seats 14A and 14B. Despite our physical proximity, we didn't know each other that well (not talking can do that to a relationship). In fact, I don't think he knew what I liked or didn't like, and I'm pretty sure he didn't know my shirt size or even my allergies. (One Christmas, when I was thirteen, he gave me an XL flannel, button-down that wasn't only too big, but also, I think from the boy section of the store.) Sometimes I teased him and asked him what my middle name was to watch him struggle with always-wrong guesses (I didn't have one), but deep down it made me sad.

We saw almost every movie that came out together: action, romantic comedies (his favorite, although he'd never admit that), drama, but never horror because he said life was scary enough. He hardly ever stayed until the end of the movie, though. He popped up during the last scene, or sometimes even thirty minutes before the credits, so he could get back to his reading chair at home. After so many years taking clients out past the point of the night where he enjoyed it, he now didn't have the patience for anything that didn't make him happy and, as such, he used his time wisely. I missed the end of many movies this way, especially the ones where he knew the ending would make him emotional. I could always tell when he was crying by peeking over at him to see if he was feeling the small hairs on the tip of his nose. When

I caught him tearing up he told me that salt had gotten in his eyes from the popcorn.

In the beginning of our friendship, when he was testing the waters of what we could share together (a daughter and a father of forty years and forty worlds apart), Dad took me to see *Casper*. The movie was meant for kids at least a decade younger than me, but he always seemed to be missing the mark on who I was or what I needed. I never said anything, though, because it seemed that Dad enjoyed that movie more than I did, the same way he loved watching *Nightmare Before Christmas* with me every Halloween, even after I stopped suggesting it (he said he sympathized with Jack). When we saw *Casper*, he cried more than I'd ever seen him before, but this time he didn't blame it on the salty popcorn.

"Dad! What's wrong?" I giggled at him when the theater lights eased on.

"It's just," he sniffled back real tears, then smirked into his affable crowd-pleasing grin. "Casper's ghost body can't feel love!" He laughed at the honesty and ridiculousness of his thoughts once said out loud. I never let him forget that moment of truth and honesty.

Movies were a way for us to communicate without speaking; enjoying the same scenes side by side silently acknowledged our mutual understanding of human sadness, humor, and existential questions. It was also the perfect way for Dad to bond with me because it didn't require actually talking. He avoided that verb so much that the only other way he could think to occupy me on the weekends was to have me chase seagulls; he promised me twenty dollars if I caught one and I later realized that a twenty-dollar bet had won him hours of free weekend time—a great trade for him. (Later in life, when kids of guests were running around his house in Maine, I overheard Dad offer a similar trade: one dollar for every fly they caught. Not only was he getting kids to stay out of his way, but he also was clearing the house of bugs, all for a very good market price.) To me, chasing birds and seeing movies was a better deal than if I let Dad choose the weekend activity, which at that point in his life seemed to be a nostalgic depression or at least a nostalgic submersion of some sort.

Most of what he taught me he did so unknowingly; I learned from watching him like an anthropologist who only studied her father. During our bimonthly visits he seemed stressed about a situation I could never see, and I consistently failed at being able to drag him into the present moment. On these weekends in Lavallette he wore the type of face that Rembrandt loved to paint, like the visages of sorrow and defeat that haunted his canvases. Whatever he felt gave his eyes a look that reminded me he wasn't listening or seeing me in front of him (of course, at that age, I'm sure my conversation wasn't the pinnacle of cerebral stimulation for him).

I caught him trying, though. Trying to be a dad. Trying to be present. In the four days a month I saw him, he was happy to give me a seemingly limitless account for food and fun. At the movies, I could have whatever I wanted: large popcorn, candy, Coke, and maybe even an arcade game. I got some of my best toys by placing bets where I controlled the outcome. I realized I could earn his respect and (even better in my opinion) his laughter by betting I couldn't finish a whole Belgian waffle during our Saturday morning diner breakfast. I perfectly buttered each square so that the maple syrup and melted dairy pooled in each nook like a creamy little sugar cube; I made my way to a Sega Genesis one bite at a time. I didn't know it at the time, but like Dad I was learning how to make trades I could win.

On his last birthday before he died I, as always, was at a loss for what to buy him, a man who had a huge house on the coast of Maine full of everything he ever wanted. I decided to buy him *Casper* on DVD. It was delivered with a note that read, "He can't feel love, Dad. But I can and I love you." Sending Dad gifts was a crapshoot, and I'm not sure if he ever watched *Casper* again or did more than laugh when he opened it, but the best gift I could think of was reminding him of our memories together, something he couldn't buy for himself. The echoes of those weekends we spent alone together were moments loud enough for me to hear, but just background noise for someone lost in the daydreams of the life he felt was just beyond him.

When I was with him the months before he died of the pancreatic cancer that saved him from dying from the ALS, we still saw movies together but we rented them on TV so we could watch them in the safety of the living room. Dad shuffled in with sweatpants and a T-shirt on, vodka and OJ in hand (unable to swallow but unable to give up his habits), and I'd hand him the remote. We were again connecting through movies, shoulder to shoulder. Dad still couldn't talk to me, but this time it was for physical reasons.

It was just like when we watched *Forrest Gump* for the millionth time (his favorite part was when Forrest put his hands on his hip and told Jenny, "I'm not a smart man, but I know what love is"). It was like that when we watched *Interstellar* for the first time, a movie about wormholes and other dimensions happening all at the same time, in the same space (he loved the scene where the main character was able to communicate with his daughter after he died in some kind of tesseract of gravity). It was here we watched the beginning of *No Country For Old Men* twice because he kept falling asleep.

Dad did invite me out to the movies a couple of weeks before he passed, way past when a doctor would advise someone on that many prescriptions to be out in a public place. The movie he asked me to go to was *Hacksaw Ridge* and I was beyond nervous to take him out of the house, morphine drip in tow, in a car and then in a theater for hours. What if he needed to use the bathroom? What if he peed in the seat? What if he started hallucinating again?

During the movie I kept stealing nervous glances at Dad, making sure he wasn't asleep, dead, or any situation that I wouldn't be able to handle alone miles from our home. But he called my bluff. This time he waited until the final scene ended and the credits rolled before getting up. He looked back to make sure I was with him and together we left the theater for the final time.

1975:
FOUR FOOLS IN
TWO TUBS

Created from the memories of
Bill McCauley, recounted over wagyu steak
at his home in Delray Beach, Florida.

I still have the last photo we took of our sailboat, the *Firebird*, almost fully sunk in the middle of the ocean, one Narwal-like mast reaching for the sky at a losing angle. We took the photo from a white life raft that became our home and savior. My best friend Kevin Connors was on my right, Chris Connors, his younger brother, was on my left, and all our dreams and investments were sinking in front of us. The plan was (what people always say before telling a tale of failed plans) to be out there on the waters for a couple years, but we had only lasted six months. Because the three of us were all varying degrees of crazy, the story that led us to being stranded in a life raft in the middle of the Pacific began with a pact.

Kevin and I became fast friends during our time at the United States Naval Academy in Annapolis from 1965 to 1969. Kevin was always a wild man, and at the time he was the only Connors I knew, so I thought it was just him.

In the summer of '69, I went to live with the whole Connors family in south Boston when my first job out of the Naval Academy was recruiting naval pilots. This was a fools' errand because, unknown to any of us sequestered in the Academy walls, there was an anti-war movement going on, and the states were alive with Vietnam war protests.

(On my first day on the job I set out to recruit at Howard University when a few students saw my Fly Navy pamphlets laid out, flipped over my table and told me to get the hell out.) I met Chris Connors during a time where anyone would want to leave all the politics behind and sail the world. We were both living together under his father's roof, a JFK Cabinet member and head of the Veterans Affairs who was closer to the affairs of state than any of us.

Chris was an Irish Golden Gloves boxer at the time, and I remember walking with him to the Tam O'Shanter, a bar at Boston College, and he was just getting into (read: starting) fights constantly, which meant we all got into fights with him of course. The thing was, he always won—flattened them in five or ten seconds. He was a pugnacious Irish Catholic boy in Boston; someone said something he didn't like, and they'd be on their backs. But he won in other ways too, slipping out of harm's way with a smile and a well-placed joke that made you want to hitch your wagon to his unflappable star.

I was now fully aboard the Connors' ride. I was with Kevin in Pensacola when he got kicked out of our flight school the way Chris was getting kicked out of bars up North. But neither stopped the party. After being discharged from flight school like a maverick, Kevin bought a bar called Dirty Joe's in Florida, and quickly made it the go-to hangout for all naval aviators who hadn't broken the rules. When Chris came down to visit us, I was never sure of where I would end up.

A couple of years before our final adventure together, the three of us found ourselves in various degrees of trouble. In 1970 we were arrested in Virgin Gorda, thrown into a tiny jailhouse for the night and forced to explain ourselves in a Tortola courtroom in front of the magistrate (a man with a flowing black robe and white wig with tight curls on each side). As antiquated as the judge looked, the courtroom was even more primitive: just an open-air structure held up by four-corner posts and shaded by a canvas "roof." We had found ourselves recounting our alibi in this setting because of some minor misjudgments that involved alcohol and the laws of Britain. The judge's "Here ye, here ye in the name of her majesty, the Queen" exclamation released the rest of the cortisol in our systems as we waited to hear our penalty. As we stood in front of the unraveled scroll in the magistrate's hands, goats, chickens, and school children walked by this lawful tent without a care for our *nolo contendere* pleas.

Luckily for us the fine was "Whatever you boys have in your pockets." We turned out our totes and gave the court anything we had. We were thrown onto the streets in the Lesser Antilles with no money or plan. Chris (who I was quickly learning had an indomitable spirit with Irish charm, sheer determination, and a silver tongue) managed to talk a yacht captain into taking us back to our US island and the boat that got us there.

But that was the story of the boat that didn't sink.

Kevin continued to serve Navy pilots whiskey and fire-water at Dirty Joe's for some time but he never stayed in one place for long. Once he tired of Dirty Joe's and post-aviator reverie, he became a student at Dartmouth business school, got his MBA, went to Wall Street to work at J.P. Morgan, and started trading government bonds.

The three of us kept in touch through the years, helping each other keep our spirits alive despite the world trying to box us in. Kevin, Chris, myself, and our friend Mark (a Navy pilot who was trading zero-coupon bonds at Morgan Stanley) promised ourselves that when I got out of the Navy we would buy a boat and sail around the world. It's very likely that none of the boys thought I'd cash that coupon, but as soon as I got out of the Navy, I dialed Kevin right away.

"I know you're sitting at a desk right now at work, but I just got out."

I paused and then filled the silence. "It's time."

In 1974, after five years of saving, Kevin and I drove up and down the East Coast looking for the sailboat that would carry out our treaty and stopped when we found the sixty-six-foot schooner we named the *Firebird*. It was $50,000 and the vessel for our next lesson: you get what you pay for (not to mention a second, subtler lesson: if you push things beyond their limits, then expect them to take on water).

We bought the *Firebird* in Fort Lauderdale and brought it back to Jacksonville the minute we signed the papers. All we had to do now was pick a date; Mark and I had just gotten out of the Navy and Chris didn't have a job, so our calendars were open from the day Kevin quit his job at J.P. Morgan. For the next two or three months, we loaded up the *Firebird* with food, beer, and the nautical charts needed to sail around the world.

The night of our departure finally came; we left Jacksonville at midnight and sailed to Palm Beach with the daughter of the commanding officer of the Navy base, who we had picked up at a cocktail party the previous night. From Palm Beach, our course was to head toward the Bahamas and then Saint Thomas. Our female co-sailor only lasted until the Bahamas, partly because she realized our plan to sail around the world and partly because we had a built-in financial mechanism to keep the girls out: the rule was if you had to bring a female, you paid ten dollars the first day to the treasury, then twenty dollars the second, then thirty dollars, until you couldn't afford it. We didn't have that much money, so this system kept us in check.

By the time we reached Saint Thomas, we had been at sea for ten days, so we anchored up and dragged ourselves into a local hotel for one last night on land. The next morning, we all met in the main salon for breakfast where we also happened to meet four girls who became the four new crew members of the *Firebird*. However, because of eventual financial hardship, they had to disembark before our departure to Kingston, Jamaica.

Cartagena, Colombia, was supposed to be our next stop but Chris was a seat-of-the-pants sailor, which meant that I more than once had to use my sextant to figure out our location during the planned 600-mile run. It was set to be a good four- or five-day sail, but we were only three days out when the gales started. The winds began blowing at forty and fifty miles per hour and the seas around us rose up to thirty feet.

We were going due south from Kingston and the trade winds were strong. The prudent thing to do (we weren't at all prudent) would have been to fall off course and run down to Panama to get away from the storm, the seas, and the wind blocking our route. Chris and Kevin discussed the option and decided to continue through the storm on an old wooden ship meant for calmer waters, because they agreed that Cartagena had prettier girls than Panama.

The gale was growing in strength and by the fourth day, it was full-on tempest seas. At one point, we watched the bow of the *Firebird* climb up a wave and poke a small pinhole in the sky before nose diving down the far side of the swell. This dance continued as the waves got steeper and steeper, but never once did we change our course toward Cartagena.

After hours of this nautical roller coaster, at around three o'clock in the afternoon, the bow of the *Firebird* disappeared into the wall of the wave in front of us. The ocean split over our heads, the weight of the water breaking on top of the entire boat.

When water crashed over our heads and covered the deck like a swimming pool, we knew it was time to worry.

We watched from the cockpit as the hatch cover on the forward peak of the boat, which was slanted forward so it could take the power of the seas, ripped off completely. That lethal piece of beautiful mahogany came flying back and slammed against the window we were standing behind in the cockpit. It sounded like bones breaking, shocking us into action like a hit from the offensive guard.

We managed to grab the hatch cover before it tumbled off the back of the boat. Chris got a hammer and some nails from one of our tool drawers and angled himself to the bow of the boat, pitching headfirst into salt and swell to nail it back on. We had passed the most turbulent part of the sea and soon the waves around us simply undulated, still looming around thirty-feet high. Given the soft surge, we dropped the sails, put out a sea anchor, and prepared to assess the damage.

I went down below and saw that the water was up above the floorboards, the salon looking more like an underwater vista for local scuba divers than our home. I grabbed a snorkel and my mask and emerged on deck saying nothing to anyone. I put on the mask, let down a rope for guidance and tipped over the side, diving down to inspect its planks under these still-massive waves. Pressing my hands against the draft of the boat, I descended down three or four planks before I noticed it. Water was rushing in through huge splits in the hull of the boat. We weren't leaking; we were sinking.

There was no time for me or any of the boys to come to terms with the fact that the ocean had ripped its way into the *Firebird*; the boat would be gone in forty-five minutes.

We didn't have any modern equipment anywhere on the *Firebird*, like an EPIRB or a GPS; all we had was a VHF radio that went twenty miles out. We were one hundred miles out, eighty miles farther than our SOS signal would take us, and no one knew where we were. We were fucked.

We launched two lifeboats, one an inflatable and the other a hard fiberglass dinghy. Given the lethal situation, I remember how calm we all were. We all took some time to get out the last few items from the *Firebird* before stepping off the cabin sole.

Chris, Kevin, and I had already swum to the lifeboats before noticing Mark was still onboard. Mark had grabbed his guitar and was leaning against the boom. We watched as he plucked a few notes on his guitar, then took it by the handle and smashed it into the front mast.

It was around four o'clock in the afternoon now and we

were scrambling into these rolling boats, twenty-foot waves
still all around us. I was in the big ten-foot lifeboat and
the rest of the crew was in the other, both tied to the sea
anchor to ride out the storm. We snapped one last photo
of the *Firebird* and then lay down as best as we could in
the tiny vessels. We lay there waiting for something, but the
only thing that came to us was eventual darkness. Around
2:00 or 3:00 in the morning, exhausted from fighting all day,
I fell asleep.

An hour or so later I woke up abruptly; my plastic raft
had been lifted on top of a twenty-foot wave and I was about
to flip over while still tied to the anchor and my friends.
I shifted my weight and as soon as I got everything righted,
I asked to switch positions with someone on a sturdier
dinghy. What I didn't know was that in the other boat, Mark
was near dying of hypothermia.

We were soaking wet, and even though we were in the
tropics at nine degrees latitude and the water temperature
was in the high eighties, the wind was blasting at forty
knots against our salt-saturated skin. When I pulled myself
into the dinghy, Mark was shivering uncontrollably. For
hours we took turns hugging him while shielding our faces
and chests from the occasional flying fish.

When the sun came up later that morning, it wasn't the light at the end of the tunnel; we were instantly and uncomfortably hot and the dead fish in the boat were beginning to smell. There were days and nights of an unbroken horizon line with no land or boat to dot the Rothko dichotomy, only the occasional splatter of birds in the sky.

That second morning, as we were eating canned SPAM and passing around a measly jug of water, Chris looked at me, Kevin, and Mark and started to laugh. The wind was howling, we were still hundreds and hundreds of miles from land, and the swells were still fifteen to twenty feet high, so nothing seemed particularly funny. I remember seeing that grin of his as he said, "Can you imagine the headline on the cover of the *Boston Globe* when we get back? 'Rub a dub dub, four fools in two tubs.'"

That was the first time we had all laughed in days and this became the turning point in our survival episode; Chris's sense of humor was a critical element of our mental state during this dire situation. The second turning point was a more tangible one: a German banana boat had spotted us and brought us back safely to land on the second night at sea.

It killed Chris to later find out that we were only one hundred miles from Colombia when we were rescued.

It could have taken nothing less than a sunken ship to hold Chris back from his goal.

[Bill McCauley now lives in Delray Beach, Florida, with his wife, Sugar. They are currently sailing their sixty-foot sloop around the Mediterranean.]

> Reprint of the newspaper article
> "An Adventure at Sea—
> With A Happy Ending"
> *by Jim Morse*

The dream of four, young adventurers—three of whom were former midshipmen in the U.S. Naval Academy—perished in the turbulent waters of the Caribbean last week, but fortunately they survived to tell the story.

The harrowing drama at sea was revealed last night by the Wollaston father of two "wild Irishmen" sons who were among the quartet rescued in the 30-foot sweeps by the crew of a West German freighter.

"Actually, it was the end of a dream, but with a happy ending," said the thankful father, William F. (Bill) Connors, director of the Massachusetts regional office of the U.S. Veterans Administration.

Connors' sons, Kevin, 29, and Christopher, 26, and two companions, Bill McCauley, 29, of New York, and Mark Warner, 29, of Texas, had sailed out of Jamaica on what they intended to be an around-the-world voyage when their two-master schooner was sunk in a tropical storm.

For the next 40 hours, the four men were pitched and tossed

in the surging sea of their life raft and had given up hope of survival until they were rescued by the German ship.

Connors said his sons phoned him from Honduras to say they were in good health and would be arriving home "no later than Monday."

The three had a dream to challenge the sea and sail around the world before settling down to raise families and carve out their careers.

Several years of employment were necessary, however, because the seafarers, who by this time had been joined by Kevin's brother, Chris, decided they needed $75,000 to finance their journey.

IN FEBRUARY, with the cash in hand, they purchased a 66-foot schooner, the Firebird, at St. Petersburg, Fla., for $50,000.

After undergoing extensive repairs, the Firebird sailed out of Jamaica on Monday, July 14, flying the Irish as well as the American flag.

The Firebird was headed for Colombia, South America, which was to have been the first stop on its round-the-world voyage.

The following day, the Firebird sailed into a tropical storm, battling 30-foot waves which tossed the schooner like a cork.

As the storm continued into its third day, the Firebird began to take on water and its pumps were unable to keep up with the surging waves. Repeated distress calls on the ship's radio went unanswered.

ON THURSDAY, the 17th, it became apparent to the four men that the schooner was going to sink. They raced to inflate their life raft, and 40 minutes later the Firebird was under water and the adventurers were being tossed about the Caribbean on their raft.

Not only had they lost their $50,000 schooner, but also the $10,000 in cash which they had left behind in their rush to inflate the raft. Furthermore, while being pitched and tossed on the sea over the next 40 hours, the men became convinced they were to lose their lives.

On Saturday, the 19th, however, they were spotted and rescued 120 miles off the coast of Colombia by the freighter Minden, sailing under the West German flag, which was en route to Honduras to pick up a shipment of fruit for United Brands Co.

United Brands notified its Boston office, which contacted the Coast Guard and the Quincy police, who informed Bill Connors and his wife, Dorothy, of their sons' near tragedy.

"The people at United Brands have been unbelievable," Bill Connors said last night. "They provided my sons and their companions with clothing and medical care, and they even arranged transportation for them to return home."

The four young men left Honduras yesterday aboard the United Brands-owned Ronde, a British freighter which is scheduled to arrive at Albany, N.Y., late Sunday night.

"It may have been a foolhardy dream," Bill Connors said, "but most of us had such dreams when we were young and did nothing about them. My sons and their friends didn't succeed in making their dream come true, but at least they tried. They have that satisfaction."

"But thank God for that German freighter. Kevin told me on the phone that it was a miracle they were spotted on the rough sea."

NOW THAT the adventure is over, Connors expects Kevin to return to his job as a trader with the Morgan Guaranty Trust Co. in New York.

"I don't know what Chris will do," Connors said. "After he graduated from UMass-Boston two years ago, he worked for the MBTA, but I really don't know his plans.

"Kevin and Chris both like to battle the odds. They knew the odds were against them on their trip around the world. That's why none of the four is married (sic). They didn't want to leave any widows behind.

"They lost everything. The insurance on the Firebird was canceled when the nature of their voyage became known. But they are young enough to start again."

The Firebird sinking

1976–1986:
WE ARE ALL GOOD AND BAD

Created from the memories found in a letter from Catherine McDonough to Chris Connors.

It was Good Friday 1976 when Chris, attired as a priest, enticed me, his hometown sweetheart, and her sister, to take an Amtrak train in Boston's South Station bound for Manhattan. Everyone else on the convoy watched as three long-legged, halter-topped, platform-heeled former gymnasts in Daisy Dukes followed a cleric-collared Chris, who was carrying two cases of beer. We cozied into one of the train-car's foursome seats and laughed about our times together during my first year of college at University of Massachusetts. I liked Chris immediately upon meeting him in Amherst; his intelligence, love for the written and spoken word, impish smile, spark in his eye, and most endearingly, his completely irreverent sense of humor.

In response to the raised eyebrows from the passengers in the seat next to us, "Father Chris" quickly explained that he was delivering these three young ladies to a home for wayward girls in New York City on behalf of Saint Ann's Parish. The home for wayward girls turned out to be Trude Heller's, a nightclub on the corner of 9th Street and Sixth Avenue in Greenwich Village. It was here where we met up with the stunning likes of Kevin Connors and three other wild men. Chris's priest outfit did not hinder his enterprises at all that night. Maybe it was a sign of the times, but no news articles came out the next day headlining that a clergy-person had climbed into the pedestal cages that encircled the drinking patrons of Trude's to share the good news of the Lord with the bikini-clad dancing girls therein.

We blurred through the rest of our Manhattan evening in a stretch limo to God-knows-where, but the closing act in the wee morning hours at a delicatessen took the black-out cake. As our group of fifteen-or-so friends sat together inhaling pre-hangover Reuben sandwiches, Father Chris felt impelled to flirt with a young woman who sat alone at a table diagonally across the aisle. Unamused, she was doing her best to ignore the advances from the good father when another patron sitting nearby intervened on her behalf.

Undaunted by the clerical collar, this tall and muscular man told Father Chris to leave the young woman alone. Apparently, this interceptor underestimated Father Chris's passion for converting young women to the faith and so was a bit stunned when the verbal altercation turned physical. A western-style brawl ensued.

Tables overturned, food and punches flew simultane-ously. I stood against a wall in complete horror and delight, bewildered about how I came to be at this moment when eight hours earlier I had planned on heading home to spend a quiet Easter weekend with my parents. This brief moment of introspection and reflection ended when the mortified Jewish deli owner appeared on the scene.

"Father! Father!" he called out while running to his aid.

Naturally beside himself that a Catholic priest was taking punches in his establishment, the deli owner chastised the chivalrous stranger and ordered him to leave the deli. The owner turned to us to apologize for this treatment, gifted us more sandwiches, canceled the entire bill, and offered to make a contribution to Saint Ann's Parish.

We caught an early train back to Boston the next morning, and I was home in time for Easter Sunday dinner with my family, no worse for the wear. I was fully charged up on life like George Bailey; Chris was my Irish Clarence.

Chris was always getting everyone in and out of trouble. On the last night that he lived in the apartment next to the old Bargain Center in Quincy Square, he did both simultaneously. He hosted an apartment-cooling party that night, and after lamenting to a group of us that his slum-lord refused the return of his security deposit because of a small hole in the screen door, he tore the door from its hinge. To see justice done, he challenged his rugby team guests to legitimize the loss of the security deposit by "wrecking the place."

With a team of men used to the scrum and controlled collisions, there were more than a few noise violations and jetsam donations flying out of the windows onto the street. As sirens hummed toward us in the distance, Chris stopped everyone and took a moment to appraise the scene before giving his final direction to Quincy's large rugby captain, "Bert, put out the light." With no hesitation, his pal grabbed a nearby end table and swatted the overhead light fixture from the ceiling. In complete darkness, our mass of hooligans jointly rolled down the front stairs of his now-destroyed one-bedroom right into Chris's panel-covered station wagon. We escaped from the scene just as the heat arrived.

After a short, high-speed chase with Chris at the helm, we were pulled over on the University of Massachusetts' Boston campus by several campus police cars. Cornered and forced to stop, Chris got out to chat with the officers; the rest of us in Chris's car watched from behind the glass, never sure what was going to happen next. Surprisingly, all that happened was a conversation between the officer and Chris before he started walking back to the car. Whatever he told them was clearly compelling because we were soon on our way without so much as a warning—a clear testimonial to his command of the English language and skills as a negotiator.

Trouble and fun aside, Chris was also a lifesaving older brother to me. During my lean years as a PhD student at New York University, when I was taking life way too seriously, he swooped in and took me out on the town. He arrived on campus in his stretch limo with all his Wall Street pals and told me to get in, even though I barely had the proper attire to run with that crowd. Those snazzy Manhattan excursions were a welcome break from the monotony of graduate student life, especially since I got home afterwards with two bags of gourmet food that Chris had ordered but never consumed (at some bank's expense, I'm sure). I would feast on these provisions of steak and crab with my graduate school pals for days.

Chris was also to thank for convincing me I wasn't a lesbian (saving me a lot of time and heartache) and constantly reminding me that being alive was quite different than living. He introduced me to culture when he took me to see *Othello*, my first Shakespeare play, starring James Earl Jones and Christopher Plummer; we sat right in the fourth row. Years later he even introduced me to my future husband on another wild Manhattan evening, a man who I had not seen since my trip to New York City with Father Chris nine years earlier. Not stopping at a husband, it was Chris who used his connections to help get me my first job out of graduate school at the legendary junk bond kings Drexel Burnham Lambert.

I smile when I think of Chris. I smile when I think of that lunch we had at Harry's in Hanover Square in 1983 when the waiter called him to the bar because he had an urgent phone call. He returned to the table, stood up on his chair, and as people dropped their steak knives to look up at this steakhouse spectacle, announced to the entire Wall Street lunch crowd, "That was my wife on the phone. She called to tell me she's pregnant, and when I find the guy, I am going to kill him!"

I smile when I think of the time I challenged Chris to dance around in the World Trade Center fountain wearing his three-piece work suit and a set of bobbing Martian ears; he did it without a moment's hesitation. I smile at all those summer weekends at his Jersey Shore rental where he was trying to get away from both his on-again-off-again New Jersey girlfriend "Bayone Debbie," who was repeatedly breaking his heart and his New York City roommate who was constantly testing his obsessive compulsions by sitting naked on his leather couch. I smile thinking that he used to carry a briefcase to his job as a bond salesman, and the only thing in it was a clean shirt, underwear, and socks for the next day of work, just in case he didn't get home that night. I smile thinking of the dream Chris often shared with me during those crazy Wall Street days and nights, leaning over his wine at dinner to tell me again he was going to build a large home on the coast of Maine where he could be surrounded by friends and family. Everything Chris told the world that would happen eventually materialized.

Chris was a connector. He was the full, metal jacket. Most importantly, he was out of the closet for everything he did. We are all good and bad, but the special thing about Chris is that he was bad about the things that don't really matter and very good about the things that matter most.

[Cate McDonough is a retired financial economist celebrating life in Cazenovia, New York.]

Chapter 3

THE PRESSURE OF SHADOWS

Winter 2016. York, Maine

There were layers and layers of healthy memories permeating the house my Dad shared with his wife Emily and their two sons. It was a house I temporarily moved into when he started to show the signs of irreparable damage done by one of the two fatal diseases set upon him in the same year. And while we were in the same rooms, breathing the same fresh air as we had during the wild Fourth of July parties and our weeklong Christmas get-togethers, now the rooms and the air felt unfamiliar somehow. Dad's sickness was only a small blip in time comparatively, one that should have been outweighed by all our other happy moments, but the layer of death's permanence proved to be the heaviest.

During my previous, non-Family-Medical-Leave-of-Absence visits to Dad's house, I slept in the sole guest bedroom downstairs (the same room my Dad eventually moved into) while the rest of his newly made family were upstairs with him. The three windows in the room looked out onto the front driveway, and the room was too cold in the winter and too hot in the summer. (Dad was against turning on the air conditioning, preferring the natural breeze of an open window, which was a shame for anyone without the coveted east-facing water view.) To help me fall asleep at night, I moved my legs between the cold, soft sheets of the bed and stared at the room's oil paintings of ships in their gold-inlaid frames and the dust-free shelves of its furniture. It was a gorgeous room in a gorgeous house—the dream house and life he had worked so long to achieve. I benefited from all his hard work, both by getting to enjoy this house on the river and because I now had the siblings I always wanted.

At night when I lay in that guest room bed, studying a painting on the wall (*How could someone paint dusk reflected on the mast of a ship so realistically like that?*), I might hear in the stillness of the massive house a struggle in the bedroom directly above me, which was my little brother Liam's room. It was the sound of a grown man with hands tight around his neck, struggling to breathe against some kind of assailant. Muffled through the floors, my ears couldn't ever be sure of what was happening upstairs, so I lay and waited in the corpse position. After a few guttural moans of fear, the noise always died down, leaving me with a receding adrenaline rush and alert mind.

To soothe myself to sleep, I found quietude in bringing my mind back to the light in the oil canvas. I let my mind wander to the Russian painter Ivan Aivazovksy and how he brought light to dark waters with paint, as if someone was holding a candle behind his canvases to allow the viewer to see the true emerald glow beneath stormy seas. I would bring up the phantom sounds the next day over breakfast, I told myself, allowing my mind to relax so I could fall asleep in the heavy silence of that lonely, first-floor room.

The next morning I found out that Dad sometimes went into Liam's room to read him bedtime stories and they would both end up falling asleep in Liam's bed. I also found out that Dad had sleep paralysis, a scary name for something usually affecting people who have incessantly harassing, late-night thoughts, a general anxiety about human existence, and a fear of losing control. It made sense: Dad had spent countless central-processing-unit cycles going over real estate mistakes, future investment opportunities, and dividends from his investment in the Perfect Push-Up. Dad explained to me that he had fallen asleep next to Liam (after answering the barrage of questions that come to an eight-year-old's mind, like, "How long does it take to get to heaven when you die?" and "Does Mrs. Claus have nice boobs?") and must have had a sleep paralysis episode last night when I heard those unnerving sounds.

Sleep paralysis is like waking up from a too-light anesthesia dosage during surgery: you can't move any part of your body and you're awake but can't speak. Often you'll see phantom figures or feel a heavy weight on your chest, the sensation that something is holding you down and that, in fact, you will suffocate or choke if you don't get the gasp of air that is just beyond your closed, seemingly suffocated mouth. The harder you try to scream for the person next to you to wake you up, to shake you from this thick cobweb of immobility, the more you tense up, and the worse the webbed ropes tighten their grip on your body.

Sleep paralysis is genetic, so I was no stranger to those nights of struggle, but I felt spoiled to have not had them in years. Unlike my dad, I had finally worked out a way to escape the invisible assailant: whenever I woke under the pressure of shadows, I simply faked relaxation and tiredness, tricking my fast-beating heart to disbelieve the feeling of drowning that took over my senses. I put all my efforts into telling myself that I was calm and relaxed, even if I felt I was under pounds of water at the bottom of the sea.

The heaviness, the inky silhouettes, and the fear I couldn't move all dispersed once I stopped trying to fight against it. Once I had acted calm enough that the paralysis hyenas moved past my still body, I was free to slowly turn on my side and fall asleep. I was proud to have eluded whatever it was around me that waited to press my chest down to the floor again. I fell asleep before they could figure out I was a sheep in wolf's clothing.

Now, years later, I had returned to the house on the York River and I was the one staying in my little brother Liam's room on the second floor. Dad was currently sleeping in the guest room directly below us because he couldn't climb the stairs to get to his master bedroom anymore. When I arrived for my no-departure-date stay, after putting in a leave of absence from work, I started unpacking, laying out my T-shirts and pajamas into the small, built-in bookcases on either side of Liam's full-size bed. We were going to be roommates, two half-siblings more than twenty-five years apart.

Rows and rows of perfectly thin and colorful hardcover books were arrayed across the bookcases' wooden shelves, purchases from the Scholastic flyers teachers sent home in Liam's backpack, thin catalogs that advertised books like candy. I carefully folded each of my cotton shirts and placed them neatly on top of each other on the bottom shelf, which Liam had cleared out for me. Still treating the world as if time wasn't about to stop, I mentally noted tasks I could take on like cleaning and reorganizing the shelves for more visual space and aesthetic balance.

Liam's room was unkempt in the way an eight-year-old's room should be—dinosaur sheets balled up on the bed, books splayed open on the ground, colored pencils on an unfinished drawing, plastic LEGO men. Next to the *Ninja Bread Man* (a book I actually read one night when I was tired of trudging through *The Goldfinch*) was a small, blue container of fish food for Max. Max was Liam's beta fish, a wet pet that spent his whole life in a Plexiglas rectangle with bright blue pebble flooring and the tiniest waterfall filtration system whose calm, babbling sounds eased me to sleep at night. That sound, along with the hiss of the humidifier and soft glow of a penguin-shaped night light, made this room the perfect respite from what was going on else-where in the house, a castle in the clouds.

Liam was an angel for sharing his room with his thirty-three-year-old sister, especially since I was constantly moving things around. I set my mind on moving his large cherrywood dresser away from the window and asked him to help me (a child!) because every morning we woke up to see the hard corners of monolithic furniture instead of the beautiful York river with its tall pine guardians. I suppose I was trying to make things better anywhere I could, those things in my control. Liam's young patience was tested a second time when I decided Max needed a place to hide. I bought a SpongeBob pineapple house for his rectangle world, its cavernous pineapple interior hiding Max from view so well that we often thought he had run away.

If it wasn't for the lack of a fish body, we would have thought Max died. It would make sense because, among everything else that was going on, we forgot this pet existed at all until once every two weeks Emily or I aggressively asked Liam if he'd fed the fish, assuming he had expired in his watery home. (Of course we knew Liam hadn't fed the fish, because we hadn't, and if the adults in the house had forgotten about Max and his fish-food needs, there was a low probability that any child would remember such a boring thing among the race cars and playdates and cheese paninis and trampoline parks that filled their days.)

Max's fortitude was constantly being tested beyond just starvation. On our last trip together as a family—a weeklong jaunt to Stowe, Vermont—Liam arranged for his uncle Russ to watch Max while we were away, his maturity surprising us. We transported the small fish on a frozen black February night, the kind where you could see not just all stars but clear past to the stardust beyond them. It was cold as we walked to the car with the aquarium in hand, the vapor of our warm breath disappearing immediately and the sharp air that crept its way into our throats stinging with every breath.

On this particular winter night, all the water molecules in the atmosphere had hardened and crystallized; frigid spectators on the metal poles and pine needles were watching us from the shadows all around us. It felt risky to tempt the atmosphere's arctic hunger by carrying a sloshing rectangle of oxygen-rich, blue water outside, a warm liquid home dotted with a bright yellow pineapple as its town square. But Liam had a plan and that included us driving a fish to his babysitter. There was Max in the center of his aqua universe, floating naively inside as we tried to position his splashing world on the floor of my cold Volkswagen. During the tense ten-minute drive, we held our breath at every turn and bump, envisioning his hypothermic death on an all-weather rubber floor mat.

Max was tough, though; he had survived weeks of famine interrupted only now and then by a heavy-handed, guilt-driven deposit of flaky fish meal, which clouded his clear water with the nutrients we had so long denied him. After a forced gluttony episode, Emily and I added another line item to the "Ways Max Could Die" list that we were silently keeping in our heads, along with the log of Dad's medication dosages. Max survived that drive, but Liam sometimes still forgot to feed him, and Emily and I were often too busy downstairs with a larger dependent to offer aid. Keeping things alive was something we were all struggling with.

Lying in bed upstairs in Liam's room, with his cartoon-railroad wallpaper and map-drawing experiments, was the most peaceful I felt anywhere in the house. But I felt guilty and sad too: Dad was below us, alone in the guest room I was always supposed to sleep in.

Dad left the guest room door ajar and his light always seemed to be on; sometimes I snuck downstairs just to see if he was up and catch him walking around the room looking busy among backup oxygen tanks. He had recently confided in me, with lucidity and strained vocal cords, that nights were the worst for him. When he woke up in the middle of the night he turned on the television and all the room's lights to try not to feel alone in the big house that he once mastered from the second floor. I didn't like thinking of him like that, but sometimes I was too tired to go downstairs to check or too mindless to know what to talk about if I did find him awake.

As I listened to the calm bubbles from Max's ecosystem and watched the dimly glowing stars stuck on Liam's ceiling fade away (a forced universe for our viewing pleasure), I realized there were going to be no more startling sounds of sleep paralysis to wake me. I tried to imagine the rhythmic sound of the oxygen machine in Dad's room and hoped it was helping put him to sleep. Turning over on my side to quiet my mind, I saw Max's underwater pineapple. Max's gossamer fins were nowhere to be seen in the now-black waters, and I wondered if Liam had fed him today.

1980s:
RUNNING DOWN
THE STARS

Created from the memories of
his first wife Paula Tepedino,
recounted over Chai tea on a porch
overlooking the Hudson River.

My sister was throwing up off starboard into the angry seas. My friend from work was retching below deck in the cabin. I stood white-knuckled next to Chris who was at the helm of our chartered sailboat for what was supposed to be a peaceful Caribbean vacation but was turning into a possible Mayday. We were in bikinis and Speedos mentally prepared for a lazy, tropical sail without a worry in the world, but somewhere near the Grenadines, on a cutter that was teetering on capsizing, my only worry was how my parents would never forgive me if my sister died.

Not long before, in the summer of 1978, I was an assistant bond trader at Dillion Read where Chris was a US Treasury Bonds salesman. When you work on Wall Street, you sit at your monitor, one of fifteen identical stations lined in a row from wall to wall, and talk on the phone all day to people you never meet. Back in the '70s, we were all crammed into a room with wires hanging from the ceiling; there was minimal decor and no windows.

I remember first meeting Chris not because of anything he said but because of the way he looked at me with those steel blue eyes of his. I had to pass by his desk to bring papers to another trader I often worked with and eventually he asked his coworker, Jimmy, who I was.

"Oh, that's Paula Tepedino," I heard him answer Chris. "She's Italian, I think."

From then on he started to call me by name, and six months later he said my name at the altar. Chris was determined about a lot of things he wanted, or thought he wanted, in his life, and he didn't let anything stand in the way of getting them. Back then, that thing was me.

Chris flirted around the idea of asking me out, but I had told him I was dating someone else, so mostly he tried to convince me he was a better choice. I had been dating my current boyfriend in Brooklyn for eight years when I came home one day and straight-out asked, "Are you going to marry me or not?" He said no in so many (or little) heartbreaking words and so the next month I said yes to a date with Chris.

On our first date, Chris wore the only suit he had (the same black one he later wore to our wedding), and I wore penny loafers and an A-line skirt with a man-tailored shirt. I fell in love with his accent and with his heart and I soon left Bensonhurst to move into a studio with him on the seventh floor of a building on Fifth Avenue and 14th Street. We filled the studio with his brass bed, one couch, a television, a stereo that we played LPs on, and a dream to buy a house on the water in Atlantic Highlands, New Jersey. On September 7, 1979, not long after we moved in together, we got married and moved inland to a home on West End Avenue in Shrewsbury.

Around that time, someone at work told him about a company called Caribbean Sailing Yachts. Chris thought it would be exciting to go sailing in the Caribbean and back then it only cost $750 to rent a sailboat for two weeks, and that included food and beverages. I had never been sailing in the Caribbean and I thought it would be fun to live on a sailboat for a couple of weeks. We invited his brother, Doug, and my sister for this vacation at sea. After six months as newlyweds, we grabbed our bags and hopped on a big bird to Saint Vincent where we ran down the stars on our boat.

When the five of us (Chris and I, his brother Doug, my nineteen-year-old sister, and a single girl from work who I had brought to keep Doug entertained and to safeguard my too-young sister) landed, we immediately headed down to the dock where our thirty-seven-foot cutter sailboat awaited us. Caribbean Sailing Yachts wanted Chris to take a "test" to see if he was an able sailor, because he had decided to man the boat himself rather than hire a captain.

Although my *naïveté* (that's a fancy French word for stupidity), certainly had its benefits in my youth, at this moment it distanced me from saying, "That test seemed awfully short to determine if our captain is seaworthy enough to take us across the open ocean in this sailboat." I was too busy stocking the boat with food for our two-week trip to notice this first red flag, but we all seemed to be ignoring things, like the fact that I could barely boil water at that time, let alone know how to stock a boat. That's how we ended up with a galley of beer and vodka.

Wait, I also stocked food. Let's see. Lettuce, check. Cucumbers, check. Oranges, check. Instant mashed potatoes, check. White bread loaf, check. Pringle potato chips, check. And the perfect accouterments to Chris's beloved screwdriver drink (half OJ and half vodka): Planters cocktail peanuts, check.

Chris had fallen in love with me, an Italian girl from Brooklyn, and during our courtship we had spent many a Sunday dinner in Bensonhurst as my mom plated him linguine with clam sauce, *pasta fra diavolo*, stuffed artichoke, thick beef stew, and chicken *cacciatore* (which we called chicken catch-a-husband at the time). I may have unknowingly pulled an audible on him as a twenty-nine-year-old wife

89

who was now serving him potato chips with Whiz spread as an appetizer. *Mama, non guardare. Mi dispiace!*

Once bikinis were on, shirts were off, and crackers were stored, our single-masted cutter left the dock at Saint Vincent with a heading south to Bequia across an open and mercurial Atlantic Ocean. As with any adventure, spirits started high as tensions from work poured off our white-skinned backs. The sun above the tropic line had yet to penetrate our epidermis to allow for the base tan we needed for protection. A few hours of sun, Jimmy Buffett, and screwdrivers later, Chris got tired of manning the sailboat, so he brought me to the helm to teach me.

"I'm going to take a nap; you're in charge," he said as he walked away after a too-quick lesson. I had passed some kind of sailing test as well, it seemed.

At some point during Chris's nap, however, the wind shifted and the boat came about quite suddenly, the bow turning toward the wind. That's when I noticed the sail luffed, we lost thrust, and now we were headed in a totally different direction. What I didn't know was that besides the wind, we had also gone from calm, protected waters into a channel that led in the Atlantic, so there was a shift in water happening underneath us that, for the moment, went unnoticed. I was afraid to wake Chris up because I didn't want to leave the helm as his chosen sentinel, so I stayed put in a state of forced responsibility, galvanized by anxiety.

Chris woke up thirty minutes later, took one look around, and started asking where we were. He never got an answer, so he checked his watch and checked the waters. The horizon was undulating and the sound of the sail clanging on the mast was becoming more ornery. White caps lined the waves around us, and the swells that had rocked us lightly started to get bigger. The sky remained blue over the open Atlantic as waves as big as houses hit us around the same time motion sickness did.

While most of the girls were throwing up, Doug and I fought off nausea and fear by sitting in the bow with our feet dangling down, our fronts facing the weather ahead. As we rode it out on the prow, the salty spray on my body started to itch. As our cutter cut through choppy seas, our pink-skinned bodies went all but unnoticed; SPF was not something we had taken time to apply.

After almost three hours of riding these twenty-foot swells, we spotted land, and Chris tacked into a safe port on Bequia. We anchored and assessed damages to our skin and our bellies. It was then when I saw Chris had severe burns on his shoulders and back—the second-degree kind of burns where blisters have formed and skin is peeling. We lovingly called him "Captain Pizza Back," not knowing that years later it became his first dance with cancer.

With no fancy boat to take us to shore, we jumped off into the shallow blue waters and swam to land, running to the tree line to find aloe plants everywhere. Back in the early '80s, Bequia and the string of Windward Islands, or Lower Grenadines, were still pristine and mostly uninhabited—especially Mustique, Savan, and the Cays. So when we anchored in the Cays, there were no docks or even substantial land masses around.

The reefs and sandbars held our anchor firmly, and at night, we slept soundly on the boat in our little cove outside of Bequia, the only sailboat there under one million stars. It was easy to fall asleep to the sound of the wind blowing and vibrating the mast and lines, metal clanking together like a sole chime, heavy canvas arching and snapping under an unmoving sky.

After Bequia, we headed to Mystique. For a week and a half, we visited these lonely islands and swam in caves, snorkeled on the beach, and speared lobsters without ever seeing another person. About three quarters of the way through our trip, however, we turned on the tap and no water came out—we had run out of fresh water.

Chris took everyone aside and interviewed them about using water, specifically how and when they had used it. It took no more than ten minutes for him to find out that my friend from work had been secretly shaving her legs with the fresh water reserves. Chris and Doug blew a fuse when they found out she had broken all the rules of sailing that she was never told. The tension on our small boat was worsening as our sunburns healed.

For four days, it never rained, so we brushed our teeth with salt water and drank only Heinekens, vodka, wine, and powdered milk. In our drought intermission, my indicted friend decided to abandon ship and fly back to the comfort of the states. No one argued. We docked at Barbados and left her there at her request.

Since we couldn't restock our water supply for a few days, we brushed our teeth and showered in the salt water a few more times, unknowingly healing our sores in the process. When we finally arrived at St. Vincent after two weeks, the four of us hardly were speaking and were happy to retreat to our individual rooms at an inn. We spent the time alone, reading or sleeping or face-first in fresh-water showers.

Being married to Chris was an adventure I'll never forget, but what I loved about him most was that he allowed me to see his vulnerability, his soft heart. During our marriage, he gave me advice I will never forget ("You can do whatever you want when you decide something") and said things to me I always remembered ("Don't leave me"), but eventually it came to an end.

Chris broke my heart when he took a broker position on Wall Street. We'd had our first and only daughter, Caitlin, together and while he loved having his "pot o' gold" in his arms, I knew his new job would lead to a lifestyle that wouldn't include his new family or the softness I fell in love with. We divorced, but I don't regret the escapades of our life together; I just realized the swells he was after were too big for me.

[Paula Tepedino is a yoga teacher-trainer and wedding officiant in New York.]

1988:
OH DANNY BOY

Created from the memories of Mark Zarrilli,
recounted over burgers at Schnipper's Quality
Kitchen on Lexington Avenue.

C hris never missed a chance to grab a slice of my mom's chocolate cake for his daughter on the way down to his Shore house. My parents, Rich and Shirley, were throwing a barbeque party on Tilton Road in Brick, New Jersey, and of course Chris stopped by for the famous cake. Kids were all crabbing with nets floating in the calm waters while the adults hung back talking about work or weather. One of the kids lost a crab from his net and screamed this fact to anyone who was in hearing distance. Chris had only stopped by for the cake, but at that moment he dove into the water without hesitation and came up with the crab clenched between his teeth. "Is this the one you lost?" he said with that huge smile of his. This is how I knew Chris: a fleeting energy who stopped by and drew you into something better.

My friendship with Chris started in the city but solidified at the beach. Even though Chris and I worked together at BGK Securities in the World Trade Center, I knew the ocean-front was his true sanctuary, as it was mine. I lived near the Jersey Shore as well, so we drove together from New York City to Lavallette, New Jersey, top down with Al Jarreau or Bob Seger on the radio. We'd always stop at the same market to pick up wine and food for the weekend, but Chris never waited for change at the register because he wanted to get to the beach so badly—every minute away from the city was sand falling in the hourglass of the weekend. If someone was ahead of him in line and the total was something like fifty-three dollars, he walked in front of everyone and left sixty dollars on the counter before walking out.

Once we were both at our homes on the beach, we got to convalesce. Chris ran ten to fifteen miles a day from Lavallette to Bayhead, sweating through a gray hoodie he wore even in summer. Then later we would meet at The Crabs Claw Inn for a beer or two at dusk, before he got Italian takeout from across the street and went home to fall asleep to whatever was on HBO.

While Chris was wild in the city, at the beach he was relaxed. He wanted to give his daughter a stable home on the weekends, so he was always good at separating his time there. Lavallette was a port in the storm for Chris, and he wanted to keep it that way. He told us, "No women, no parties. I have my daughter this weekend."

Still, Chris was always on the lookout for an opportunity and he didn't take weekend breaks. Sometimes the manager of The Crabs Claw saw Chris walking in and had to tell him, "Don't bother coming in tonight, Chris; there are no new waitresses for you this week." Chris had tried to date all of them. I remember because I was next to him for most of those attempts—Chris leaning over to tell me he was going to turn his blue eyes way up before walking over to the girl.

Despite getting arrested one summer for skinny-dipping in the ocean and spending the night drunk and nude in jail, most of our days and nights were tame. No one in Lavallette knew the legends of Chris, so for the most part he flew low and he flew solo.

Our lives with our families at the Shore were the ebb before a week on Wall Street, where we'd both put on suits and a smile and trade our health for money. But regardless of latitude, wherever he was, Chris was always the nucleus of action.

At work, he had a diverse group of friends, not just those Ivy League monotone groups you often see in our field. Chris didn't care if you went to Harvard; he just wanted to know if you were an asshole or not. In fact, it was okay if you were an asshole too, as long as you owned up to it.

Chris was a mentor and a close friend to me while we worked together in the '80s. Besides being fun, he also had a huge heart (when I won the Wall Street charity bout heavyweight division, Chris and the partners won big on my fight and Chris made sure I got some of that money). I'm not the only one who loved Chris; he always had a *Playboy* and Scotch in his desk drawer, so I'm not sure if there was anyone outside of human resources who didn't like him. HR couldn't keep up. We were allowed to have "happy birthday strippers" come to the office floor at work. On slow days, Chris asked the floor, "Whose birthday do you want it to be?" and before lunch, we'd have girls dressed as gorillas, cops, and mailmen making their way through the cubicles.

Chris's best friends were usually clients too, and that was the case with Tony (or Dr. Woo, as we called him), who was shot as a teenager in Chinatown and lost the tips of his fingers in a knife fight. Chris preferred that type of seasoned crowd over ironed button-downs, which I suspect is why he kept me around. I was a Jersey Shore guy, and one of considerable size. He may have kept me around just because I was the biggest guy at the bar. Chris loved the fight and it was more likely that some drunk wanting a challenge would look our way for poking and prodding when I was around. Unlike skinny Chris, however, I hated bar fights and, to his dismay, kept us out of more than a few brawls he knew I could win.

In Chris's younger days, though, I wasn't there to keep him out of trouble. He told me of the time he and his brother, Doug, went to a bar and Chris went to the bathroom, took off all his clothes, and left them in a pile on the floor near the toilet. He emerged into the packed bar completely naked and ran across the top of the bar and jumped across table tops until he was chased out. As he ran out the front door, he crashed chest-first into a cop car that was parked outside. When Doug finally came out of the bar, Chris was still naked, handcuffed, and bent over the cop car. Doug claimed he was Chris's lawyer and demanded that the officer release him immediately. They were both handcuffed and taken to jail.

That wasn't the first time Chris was chased out of a bar either. Before I met him I had heard that Chris and two of his friends snuck into a live music bar and claimed they were an Irish singing group. They were dragged off stage and into the street before the end of their first rendition of "Danny Boy." When I retold him this story upon meeting him, he simply said, "Mark, do as I say, not as I do,"—a warning I kept close during nights I ended up keeping him out of more trouble than he knew what to do with.

Chris and I bonded over the calmness of the beach

as much as we bonded over the opportunity Wall Street
afforded to blue-collar men who were in the right place
at the right time. On the nights we didn't have to take out
clients, Chris and I went to P.J. Clarke's for burgers and
a Bass Ale and then to the movie theater a block from
his Lexington Avenue apartment. Chris loved movies,
and he saw anything that was out, even the sappy ones.
I remember looking over at him during Jack's speech in
Titanic, but when I asked him if he was crying, he said
he just had salt in his eye from the popcorn. He was
getting salt in his eyes during the end of lots of movies,
I noticed.

After he retired from finance, leaving a palatable
absence in the mushroom-cloud aftermath of his thirty-year
detonation, Chris called all his friends randomly while they
were still at work. When they picked up he told them about
a joke he had just heard, asked them what the two-year
yield was, or retold them about his recent courtship with
death in Russia. Then, suddenly, he would say, "I gotta go,"
and hung up—he was always a tornado like that.

Chris was stingy with his time and so he did the sudden goodbye when it came to going to bed early. He started to leave bars and restaurants earlier and earlier as he grew older. He'd get a burger and a vodka OJ to go from P.J. Clarke's, then leave both by his bed almost untouched before passing out (I know because I spent many nights on his couch). If you were at his house in Maine, the ending of the night felt similar: he'd eat a late dinner (usually rare steak and mashed potatoes, finished with a glass of cold milk and a cookie) and would tell whoever was sitting at his dining room table, regardless of if they were mid-conversation, "I love you guys; I'm going to bed."

When I was out with Chris and a group of friends on the East Side, he side-doored as usual around midnight. The next day we all found out that on his walk home he had tried to stop a woman from being mugged and ended up getting stabbed in the back of the leg. He tried hailing a cab to Bellevue Hospital, but no cab would pick him up because he was bleeding everywhere. No matter what happened in the group after Chris left, he always got the last story. If you weren't with him, you were likely missing some kind of action that sniffed him out, whether he wanted it or not. I wasn't with him all the time, and I wish I could have gotten him out of a few capers I missed. But I couldn't protect him from his worst assailant, and I'll think about that for the rest of my life.

[Mark Zarrilli recently retired from Wall Street, wrote a book about his life called Brick and Mortar, and bought a house in Lavallette, New Jersey in the memory of his best friend.]

Chapter 4

5:15 A.M./P.M.

Winter 2016. York, Maine

December approached Rams Head Lane with the chill of something worse on its tails. Dad was waning, the boys were growing, and Emily and I were running on stress and Syrah as the rest of the world prepared for the holidays. The mail was dropped off in string-tied bundles on the front porch of the capacious wooden home, a home that was getting fewer visitors every week but more and more glossy Christmas family photo postcards—a strange tradition, if you think about it.

Humans do a lot of strange things we never question: we create imaginary lines across land, put meaning in the stars that dot our night sky, get high off fermented potatoes, kill flowers just to attempt to keep them alive in stagnant water for us to admire, take trees from outside and burn them in our homes, and throw what's in our homes into landfills where there should be trees. But this particular peculiarity of sending out holiday cards meant that this year our family had piles of photos of other families, snapshots of lives that were continuing outside of death's waiting room.

We'd set each card in a pile on a counter somewhere with the intention to hang them later, as we did every year, but the truth is that the pile was just another one of the visual to-dos that were slowly multiplying all over the house. And while friends and family begged to help in any way during this "hard time," all we could think to ask for was more casserole dishes of lasagna, a meal we may never be able to eat again, according to the psychology of association.

Normally (that is to say, when someone wasn't dying in the house), Emily took the cards and taped them to the deck doors on either side of the kitchen, displaying a tangible and overwhelming example of how many relationships she was able not only to keep up, but to keep flourishing. Sometimes she got so many cards there were too many for two full-sized glass doors and she had to start overlapping edges or start using some wooden columns in the house. Emily was a master at relationships and had a way of nurturing, listening, and calling (with a phone, to have actual conversations about details you forgot you had even mentioned to her months ago) that made you feel as if she was yours alone. Everyone around her felt her full love and attention, and I never figured out how she managed to do that with so many people, the way the symmetry at Arlington cemetery makes you feel as if all the tombs lined up only for you, as if the landscape was built around you as its center. By the looks of Emily's kitchen in December, she had enough close friends to remind us that we'd never have to make another lasagna again.

Her kitchen also sullenly reminded me of the empty kitchen in my Philadelphia apartment. I found myself comparing my life to hers; maybe I would get holiday cards like these when my friends and I were able to acquire the things worthy to photograph for the card, like puppies and babies and husbands. A holiday card of me standing next to my utility bills on a couch I got off of Craigslist while holding a McDonald's bag hardly elicited the feeling of a Hallmark Christmas movie.

For the past five or so years I had mixed feelings of happiness and distance when I got Emily and Dad's holiday card in the mail, sent to whatever new Philly apartment I had signed a twelve-month lease for. There was a picture of their two boys, my half-brothers Liam and Chris Jr., and their two shih tzus, Bam Bam and Woo Woo (named after Dr. Woo, a mysterious man named Tony Wang who my Dad used to hang out with in Lavallette on the weekends). The printed signature on the cardstock read, "Love Chris, Emily, Little Chris, Liam, Caitlin, Woo and Bam." I was so surprised the first year I saw my name on the card, like being adopted into a family I always hoped I would have. Except it was my family, kinda.

I felt sad at the same time—sad to know I wasn't living in the warm security of their home but just visiting temporarily. I lived paycheck to paycheck. I was out of the nest and, as the daughter of divorce, I had no childhood room to go home to when things got tough. But Dad was training me to be tough; his hard lessons for me in character building included a two-week Outward Bound expedition that involved surviving alone in the wild and learning to sleep on rocks without a pillow or blanket, an experience that I broadcast in my college application essays.

In Emily's warm kitchen I pushed aside all the holiday cards that never got hung that year and I realized this holiday that I was with them, all together under one roof like the card's signature implied. Everything was perfect. Except for the fact that I was losing my father right when I was finally gaining one.

Emily and I thought it would be cute this year to buy matching, reindeer-studded long johns for this year's family Christmas photo. Of course we also got a set for the dogs of the family: the two French bulldogs, Lola and Mongo (a dog my Dad named after Mongoloid from *Blazing Saddles*); a massive golden retriever "puppy" named Ruger (whose extra skin and fur slouched side to side as he walked, signaling that in time he would grow to be a huge werewolf); and my Shiba Inu Doge-in-the-flesh named Bambi, whose general malaise and disregard for dogs confirmed that she was a high priestess in a past life. The five of us and the four dogs were all dressed in these tight, unattractive pajamas on a day we planned and we sat perfectly for someone to take our photo; the last holiday card we had together (and the first).

Dad had insisted we not cancel sending a card this year, even though I had a hard time finding a fitting template online. *The Best Year Ever* written in silver wouldn't work, and the glittery *Joy* was so un-Connors that our mailing list would assume it was a kidnapper's humorous way to let everyone know we were tied up and no longer allowed to correspond with the outside world. There was also the question of how skinny Dad had gotten and the idea that it could be a shocking visual for some people to receive without a warning that he was very sick. Plus, I had no idea what to write, having decided Dad's suggestion of "By the time you get this, I'll be dead" could also rub people the wrong way, a favorite pastime of his.

We decided on some text that involved curse words and asked a friend if he was free to take our photo on Wednesday at 7:00 p.m. We washed and folded everyone's long johns and placed them in each person's room on their dresser, even though Emily and I were the only active adults in the house who knew or cared what folded items on a dresser signified.

The photo appointment was soon canceled in lieu of hospice visits, dinner preparations, random bloody noses (despite the house having a humidifier in every room), and Ruger's monthly stomach bug. (We called it a bug because of cognitive dissonance; the reality was each of us separately had stepped on some kind of foamy spit pile that may or may not have included too-large pieces of human food, plastic parts of LEGOs, and a whole sock that had made its dark journey through the canine intestines and back.) The weeks went on, days vacuumed up by routine and emergency, and in the back of our heads we knew the to-do piles were getting bigger, Dad was getting smaller, and a holiday card at this time was a bit zealous on our part.

We all scurried about the house consumed by our own sched-ules and inner agenda; we all had our daily routines and Dad didn't want to be left out of that bustle. He tried to get back into his own daily routines but they were escaping his neurodegenerative grip more and more as the winter picked up speed. When Dad was healthy (and not doing some bucket-list item that brought him to Russia or Alaska), he cycled through his daily routine without fail. A normal day went something like this: wake up early and turn on the speaker in the kitchen to 92.5 The River, get a glass of chocolate protein smoothie (pre-made by Emily every morning), retreat to his office to read *The Onion* or *Al Jazeera* on his computer, email funny links to a group of people currently at work in a cubicle (a place of business not happy to receive whatever NSFW picture was currently pixelating through an outer space satellite about to land in their corporate inbox), take an afternoon nap, make a grilled cheese, grab his hardcover copy of *Rough Riders: Theodore Roosevelt, His Cowboy Regiment, and the Immortal Charge Up San Juan*, and sit in his red reading chair next to the fireplace before making a vodka OJ around 5:00 p.m., showering again, turning on *Family Guy,* and waiting to be beckoned by Emily to start the hell-fire industrial grill out back that no one wanted to touch for fear of miscalculating the fragile process of meat incineration.

When Dad got sick, the time and schedule we understood started to become blurry for him. Miraculously and strangely, some of his previous daily routine lingered in a part of his memory and must have mutated into new weird actions in his last days. Watching him stand in front of the smoothie-filled blender hitting "pulse" for a good deal longer than anything on this earth needed to be pulsed, only to then walk back into his room consumed by a new hallucination, meant he lost himself long before we did.

Whatever drug-induced hallucinations and thoughts Dad had, it was Emily and I who had to watch his new confusing practices. His brain synapses were now catalyzed by these new insidious reflections of daily patterns that were beginning to disperse into the darkness of the mind where all memories disappear. It was especially hard to stop him from clinging to those specifically human tasks our days drown in under the endless forward motion of the hour. So we let him pretend his days were routine. We watched him get dressed in blue jeans even though he was only awake now for two or three hours. We positioned ourselves near him as he tiptoed on the fireplace ledge, clinging to the mantle with one hand and with his free hand trying to wind a brass Chelsea Bell ship clock that had stopped at 5:15 on a day that no one could remember. However, his afternoon reading-turned-nap sessions were a respite in a day of anxiety, and we were glad that part of his routine stayed with him.

He was happy (a word we labeled him with, not knowing what exactly he felt now) in that chair with a lap full of *Guns & Ammo* magazines and his pharmacy-bought reading glasses sitting proudly on the bridge of his freckled nose. There in the center of the house, we could keep an eye on him while continuing with our day. His reading chair faced the interior of the living room, front door, and kitchen, its red-cushioned back facing a gorgeous water view that he had spent time and money on creating for his guests to look at while he faced away. All the action in the house seemed to face him in this position, a one-recliner audience member watching the stage he had set in his house. In this way he was able to read but also look out above the top of his pages to see what his troupe was up to, people he loved having around him but who he also enjoyed watching from a distance. He loved knowing we were nearby and was comfortable knowing that the ecosystem he created didn't always need to include him.

One November day as we all went about our errands and peculiarities, we almost missed something very important that happened during one of Dad's attempts to regain a semblance of normality. Dad shuffled out of his first-floor bedroom to sit in his reading chair, when Emily and I noticed it. Instead of jeans or gray, drawstring sweatpants, this 130-pound lanky leaf was dressed head to toe in tight reindeer long johns, the ones that had sat folded on top of his dresser for weeks (something we had placed there for us to remember rather than in the hopes he recognized anything in his room). He sat down in his chair in pajamas that had red elastic ankles and wrists. I nudged Emily in the kitchen because I couldn't take my eyes off of the lion of a man, the Wall Street tornado, the boxing champ, the looming and distant rock of a dad who was now walking unassumingly into the living room, magazines under his arms and reindeer on his ass.

Only a year ago, Emily had asked Liam to go upstairs and put on his similarly cartoon pajamas when my dad looked him straight in the eye and asked him what kind of man he wanted to be, "Do you want to go upstairs and put on those girly pajamas or stay down here and eat sugar until you fall down like a champ?" Now here was that same Dad, following the rules he taught us to break. It was as if time had stopped as I watched him sit down, his back toward the view we loved, waiting to see if he was going to say something about his ridiculous new outfit. He sat for a few moments, then got up and faced the fireplace before reaching one long and bony arm up to the mantle, chicken leg bent in order to step up onto the stone ledge.

As he tinkered with the frozen-in-time ship clock to no avail, I did exactly the thing I hated when I saw Dad's visitors do it: I infused the situation with forced meaning. I knew they were turn-ing his final days of mental dissolution into meaningful messages to make themselves (or us) feel better. Now, I read into Dad's abhorrent fashion choice the message that he wanted to have this last Christmas card done before he left us. And so we all slipped into our droopy-crotched Christmas long johns, besieged each of our own unsuspecting or sick dogs, and swarmed to the fireplace for a quick, unprofessional photo in front of a timed, propped-up phone. I begged everyone to "look" and "smile" and watched as the flash sped up and released to capture our first and last holiday card photo together; one last shot capturing a life before time stopped.

1993–2012:
THEY'LL HAVE TO
FIND ME TO FIRE ME

---

*Created from the memories
of Mike Kenny, recounted over a
forty-four-ounce porterhouse for two at
Wollensky Grill on Third Avenue.*

To this day, my wife says her least favorite years of my career on Wall Street were when Chris Connors and I worked together, a friendship that spanned over a decade.

Chris was credited as the man who invented limo surfing, an initiation for brokers on Wall Street to stand on the roof of our corporate limos as they barreled down the streets of New York City. He was well-known as the "maniac bonds broker" on the Bloomberg grapevine long before our paths finally crossed. In the '80s he had been limo surfing, fighting people in bars and getting stabbed on the street, but we didn't become friends until the '90s at Donaldson, Lufkin & Jenrette, now Credit Suisse. Once we started hanging out together, it became very bad for my liver but very good for my life.

It was mostly easy being a bonds salesman: just pick up the phone and don't drop it. In the age before email, when business was done with a phone call, egregious Chris became everyone's favorite salesman, not to mention everyone loved his Boston accent. He was also competitive and, because I had a little more acumen for the analytic side of the business, every once in a while he got serious and asked me to teach him something.

Sitting at our desks on quiet afternoons, I explained bond prices, yields, duration, and interest-rate derivatives. Some clients, like Neeraj B., knew what they wanted to do and didn't need Chris to determine if there was some analytical algorithm to it (Neeraj would just call him and say, "Chris-o, buy me two million ten-year notes."), but Chris wanted to have a working knowledge of what he was doing. We'd have these funny little thirty-minute teaching sessions and then we'd all go out drinking and forget the day.

I remember the day I tried to teach him about repos and match sales. Every morning at 11:30 a.m. the Federal Reserve opened markets and the desk announced what they were going to do in the market that day—either add money to or drain money from the system, depending on if they wanted to slow down the economy or give the economy some juice. They used to call it Repurchase Agreements; they'd go into all the banks and buy securities, in essence taking the bank securities and giving them money in exchange so that the banks could have more money to do what they do best: lend more. The economy would be more stimulated.

Conversely, if the Federal Reserve thought the economy was growing too quickly, they did reverse repurchases, where they made the dealers/banks buy securities from them, taking money off the banks' balance sheets so the banks had less money. Whether it was a repurchase or a reverse repurchase, the Federal Reserve did what they could to fine-tune the market, doing whatever they thought was the right path for money supply and economic growth.

One day Chris looked at me and said, "Repo, reverse repo—cut the crap, what does this mean?" I explained as best as I could, as I just did now, and the next day he had a single, yellow Post-it on his computer screen that read, "Repo GOOD. Match Sales BAD."

At DLJ, there was an antagonistic relationship between the traders and the salesmen. Chris and I leveraged this to organize a trader-versus-salesman basketball game in the basement of our building; both sides spent the day betting on who would make the shots. Chris was my finance backer so he asked me, "Mikey, are you sure about this one?" and I'd let him know I could make the shot from anywhere on the court, no problem. The traders bet $100 on me and then Chris upped the ante.

"$100? You guys are supposed to be big risk-takers! Come on, I've got $5,000 on this." We challenged the youngest traders with the biggest egos, and we never lost.

After one game, one of the young traders looked at me all sad and said, "I just lost way more money than I have in my account." That's when we taught him a valuable Wall Street lesson: don't miss the shots you can't afford.

And boy, did we take as many shots as we could. Our boss at the time had hired a bunch of other lunatics who just wanted to party, and it seemed that was what Wall Street was paying us to do. Sometimes our boss came out of his corner office and would say to the whole floor, "Go. Get out" demanding we go take out clients in order to get their business.

"If five of you don't get up and leave right now, I'm going to start firing people."

I was forty years old; these guys were in their thirties and early forties, and even though Chris was the senior statesman among us, he made sure we were out until the bitter end of the morning. If we left our desks at noon, that meant Chris was having wine during the day and vodka and orange juice throughout the night.

The market was great, and we were all making a ton of money so things got a little crazy. One morning, after our group had been out destroying all night, a coworker came into work, sat across from us and looked across the desk, saying only to himself, "Someone's got to tell his firm the '80s are over." Our boss encouraged us, though. An expense report line item for six hours and $3,000 got a no-questions-asked approval.

Except for the times Chris asked me to explain finance intricacies to him, he never much cared about learning bond math—his whole passion was just engaging with people. His clients knew what they wanted to do, so they asked themselves, "Should we do it with Chris or with some asshole who worked at Goldman Sachs who thinks he's a nuclear physicist?" They all did their trades with Chris Connors because they loved him and he treated them like true friends, because that's what we all became. And that's what sales was about back then: personal relationships, entertaining, and having a ball together.

Five or six times while working together we got to take our favorite clients to the Super Bowl. We chartered boats to throw pre- and post-Super Bowl parties on, all the while being praised that we were great at our jobs. One of the first, big Super Bowls together was in Miami. Having no interest in standing in the din of the stadium all day, we chartered a boat during the game; we were all drawn to the beach after sitting in cubicles all day.

We had brunch at the Loews Hotel that morning of the charter when Chris started chatting up an older couple whose very attractive daughter was sitting with them, covering her bikini'd body with only a fishnet dress. Tiffany. Turns out they were in Miami for an antique show (on Super Bowl weekend). Chris asked the couple if he could take the daughter on the boat with us, and of course the father was suspicious, but Chris assured him we'd take good care of her.

"That's what I'm afraid of," her dad replied before agreeing with a salesman who could sell ice to an eskimo.

We brought Tiffany to our boat party and she was like a zebra at the watering hole surrounded by predators, but no one else got any time with women around Chris. I talked so much that they'd get sick of me while Chris sat there quietly and smiled, and they were always drawn to go sit near Chris. He was very lovable that way.

Once in a while, we'd get tickets to a big concert at the Meadowlands, rent a huge party bus, and load it up with booze and food. We'd invite everyone (clients included for expense reasons) so that there'd be this mishmash of young girls, young brokers, old farts like Chris and me, and all sorts in between, just partying and raging on the way to the concert and on the way back to the city too. And even when we got back we'd then stay out even longer in Manhattan as if we hated our mattresses.

When Bruce Springsteen was playing at the Giants Pavilion, we all took our spots outside our office waiting for the party bus as per our usual preconcert tradition. But this time when the bus pulled up and the door opened, Chris walked out in full-blown Dr. Evil makeup, bald cap, fake scar, and head-to-toe gray costume. It wasn't Halloween. Everyone dropped their cases of booze and conversations and were in tears laughing.

He stayed in that costume for the full Springsteen concert. But on the bus ride home everyone really was getting out of control. People were dancing, cute girls were making out all around us; it was Sodom and Gomorrah, but Chris was sitting on a bus seat away from it all looking down, his hair covered with skin-colored latex, his cheap makeup sweating white streaks everywhere. I went over and sat down next to Chris and put my arm around him as he explained no one would dance with him.

"I picked a pretty stupid day to dress as Dr. Evil," he said.

It wasn't just the clients and partiers who loved Chris. The head of quantitative research at DLJ at the time, a brilliant man and very successful trader at Blackrock, fell for him as well. He'd come down to have some laughs with Chris because he'd been out all day with the research team, who were all brilliant at splitting the atom but weren't a whole lot of fun. During one of these visits, he asked Chris what reports he was working on and Chris simply said, "Well, I got these," as his right hand opened a desk drawer full of *Playboy* magazines. It was the levity we all needed in a sea of tickers, numbers, charts, and egos.

When Chris was with me listening to a buddy of mine, a brilliant man with a Master of Business Administration from Columbia University and a PhD in psychology, he wasn't swayed by his Harvard-graduate renaissance man talk. When we were together, this guy was in the middle of talking about Freud, and Chris would just stop him and say, "What are you even talking about? Have a vodka!" He relaxed people like that. Instead of pretending to keep up, he set the speed.

Chris could engage anyone, so every day working with him was full of laughter.

"Mike, there's this wicked hot bah-maid at Alfredo's," he said to me randomly. Alfredo's was this touristy restaurant by Rockefeller Center, and Amanda was the adorable bartender caged up there. By all stretches of the imagination, it was a boring restaurant, but we had a big customer dinner coming up, so we decided to bring our group of ten there rather than our usual wine-and-dine spots simply because of a cute bartender. Chris was an adventurer and sometimes that meant creating his own waves.

We booked a business lunch at kitschy Alfredo's, a gimmicky Italian spot that attracted the kind of cruise ship crowd that Chris described as "overfed, newlywed, and mostly dead." When we got there, Chris gave the owner money to play Led Zeppelin over the loudspeakers. Amanda and Chris made sure the alcohol was flowing, and the next thing we knew it was 3:00 p.m. in the afternoon and we had everyone in the restaurant dancing on tables to "Good Times, Bad Times." Outside on the streets, all of these tourists were walking by this cheesy restaurant and looking in to see the whole place singing, "In the days of my youth." We had always had a tendency of turning boring around.

Over the next twenty-five years, I watched Chris fade away from Wall Street. He showed up less and less often for events, instead going to Maine almost every month to work on the house he was building or to see the waitress who later became his last wife. Once he found Maine, his house, and his love, that's all he cared about. He never looked back, and he had no regrets—I know that for sure.

One night Chris came down from Maine and sat with me for dinner at Smith and Wollensky, and I could tell he just couldn't handle the city swells anymore. It was that night over steak and seafood (I never ate seafood before I met Chris; I was just a mutt from Yonkers eating steak every night) that he said, "I love you guys, but I can't wait to get back to Maine." He was starting to say goodbye to us. "I don't miss the city anymore."

December 22, 2002, was his last day at work, but he was the only one who knew that. I had been sitting next to him for years, and at the end of each day he would say, "Mikey, love you, baby" and head out until the next day. On this day he pushed back his chair, got up and said, "Mikey, love you, baby. Have a good Christmas."

"You too, Chris-o. See you after New Year's. Enjoy Maine."

"I'm not coming back."

"What do you mean? Like until January 5?"

"No, I'm not coming back ever. I'm done. I'm out of this business."

"Well, are you gonna tell anybody?"

"They have to find me to fire me," Chris said.

He continued to get checks from the company for another four months.

When I called Chris a few years after he retired to talk about him coming back down to NYC for a big dinner with all his friends, I could hear that his voice was starting to slur from the ALS that not even he knew he had. I regret not catching it sooner, but he was drunk so often in our friendship that sometimes on the phone he slurred a little bit and I didn't think anything of it. Chris had a heavy accent, so throw a little booze in there, a little tiredness, and you wouldn't have noticed that his enunciation was any different than when he got ALS.

The last time I talked to Chris was November 2016. I said I was going to come up to Maine to visit him.

"Mikey, don't bother," he said with a very labored voice. "The ALS doesn't have a chance; the pancreatic cancer is going to come for me before the ALS."

That conversation was a month before he died.

I should have just gone up to see him, but you never know with Irish guys if they mean it or don't mean it. My wife says that I deal terribly with death—I internalize, I don't want to be hugged—but to this day, I can't believe I didn't just go up, despite Chris saying, "Don't botha. I'm getting tired just talking to you on the phone."

Chris and I were similar in that way—we have to be strong in public, but it doesn't mean we're not emotional, that we don't feel it. But I learned two things the day Chris died: that it takes the death of a best friend to make an Irishman cry, and it takes two fatal diseases to kill one.

[Mike Kenny lives a life of mystery and cannot be found at the time of publishing. He loved Chris Connors dearly.]

1992–2010:
I WOULD

Created from the memories of
Chris L. and Neeraj B., recounted over bacon
cheeseburgers, cooked medium rare, and
fries at Corner Bistro in New York City.

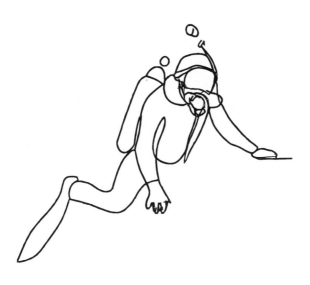

We had heard the fairy tales, the fantastical bedtime stories of '80s Wall Street when people didn't sleep, girls were riding in limos everywhere, and the office was just a place where you ate your lunch. (*Wall Street, Other People's Money, Bonfire of the Vanities,* and every other Wall Street movie of note was set in the late '80s for a reason.) But we didn't know how true they were until 1992, when we were a bunch of twenty-four-year-old babes in the (more tame) woods. That's when we met Chris, our connection to the era of those wild times.

We were traders just starting work at J.P. Morgan and Chris was someone we chose to trade our government bonds with because he was so different from anyone else we talked to. Everyone else was aggressive—you felt like they were trying to get something out of you, pressing how smart they were upon you in order to push their agendas. Not Chris. Chris was the nicest, most genuine guy in the world. Even if you didn't trade with him for a month, he didn't care; he genuinely wanted to see you, know about your life, and how you were doing. He was making real relationships in a world where everyone was undervaluing people.

We were his clients, but it didn't take long for the relationship to change, and he became like a father figure (or naughty uncle) to us, our guide in the world of Manhattan. He taught us how things really worked, the rules of the games: how many nights of the week you can go out; that we don't go out on Monday, but go hard Tuesdays and Thursdays; that you should always start drinking beer around 11:00 p.m.; that brown liquor was bad and clear was good. He was teaching us the ways of the world, the Wall Street world, from the eyes of a grizzled veteran.

He mentored us for years, clearly explaining to us what was going on on the other side of the phone when we called. If we did a business transaction with Chris, he said, he was really representing a number of other people within the bank he was working at. He said we were only talking to him, but there were a bunch of other people ultimately facing the consequences of whatever we did. He was the first person to explain what a trader's life was like and why we should care.

He didn't do things the way anyone else did, so it's fitting that Chris got his first, big client in a way no other can lay claim. He was working for a securities firm in Boston and was having trouble getting a Rolodex that could sustain a career. There was a woman in charge of a pension fund who would have been a great first client, but his boss at the time told him there was no way she'd agree, joking, "You're just gonna have to date her." Chris thought that made sense, so he did; he started dating that woman, and she became his first client.

Doing business with Chris became easy once we became friends, because trading with him meant going to his favorite place: restaurants. He loved eating, and he loved it even more surrounded by people he cared about. Client dinners were a five-night-a-week thing sometimes. Whenever we'd meet Chris for dinner, we'd usually be almost an hour late (business, traffic, happy hours). But as consistently as we were late, he was early to the reservation. Whenever we finally arrived, we'd find him sitting by himself at the best table in the restaurant, waiting with two bottles of wine and a grin. In New York City, especially at the good restaurants, no one will seat you unless your whole party has arrived, but Chris always went into these places and worked his charm. (We overheard once that the conversation went something like, "Listen, my people are coming. What I'd like to do is sit at your table and order two of your most expensive bottles of wine, and if that's okay, I'd like to be able to do that right now.") As good friends, we sometimes even went out with him to his favorite late-night (read: early morning) place, P.J. Clarke's. After hours of drinking and entertaining, he'd stop at P.J. Clarke's and order a cheeseburger at the bar before heading to his apartment. We were vegetarian for years except when we went to P.J. Clarke's to eat a hamburger with Chris and, later, in honor of Chris.

Those dinners and expensed meals ended in close bonds and shared personal stories, but they always started with some light work talk on our part. Whenever we'd ask Chris for his advice about if we should take a deal or not, he didn't waste time with a pretentious explanation of why we should move forward and ink the trade; he simply paused and then told us, "I would." That laconic phrase eventually popped up as his answer for subsequent and aberrant situations, including but not limited to: if you should go skinny-dipping at a party, if you should donate enough money to the Leukemia Society to be able to run the Boston Marathon five times despite never qualifying, if you should go snowshoeing in Russia to hunt black bears, or if you should ask the girl out. Chris's "I would" held the same galvanizing effect as 9/11's "Let's Roll" (which Chris later named his thirty-six-foot Sabre motoryacht) or the more traditional "hold my beer."

Would you ask to be invited to the wedding of someone you didn't know just because of the destination and then take newbies into a dangerous situation without the proper guides?

"I would."

The time he taught us how to scuba dive during a wedding he wasn't originally invited to was when our friend Julian's twin brother was getting married in Bali. Though Chris had only met the brother once, their brief interaction manifested into a wedding invitation halfway across the world. After receiving the invite, Chris talked his company HSBC into buying him a ticket all the way to Bali because he said it was for work.

After going out all night in Bali on the first night, we just wanted to sit around and do nothing all day. Chris really liked scuba, though, so he got up early in the morning before anyone was up and drove the ninety minutes across the islands to go diving by himself. When he returned and invited us to go with him the next day, we told him we had never been diving before, hoping this ended the conversation.

Chris, a good salesman, was prepared with a rebuttal.
"It's okay," he said. "I brought back some scuba gear from
today so I can teach you in our pool." If you've never been
in a villa that has a pool, know that they're usually about
three-feet deep and hardly bigger than a bathtub; you
can't get your head under water if you try.

In a few hours we were bobbing in a shallow villa pool,
loaded up like Marines with our scuba mask, buoyancy
compensation device (inflatable vest), a scuba tank, dive
weights, a regulator, and fins.

"Just lie on your back" he kept saying as we turned like
logs in a flume.

We finally balanced ourselves enough to lie on our
backs with the gear for about one minute, trying not to flip
over or pull a wrong tab, when suddenly Chris exclaimed,
"You're good!"

"Chris, we don't have a diving license," we protested
as we watched him start to pack the car for our morning
ocean voyage.

"You don't need a license," he said calmly. "You're
with me."

The next day, armed with a fifty-dollar bribe and a
bathtub certification, Chris took us diving in the open water

for the first time. Chris was up for anything, always taking the opportunities that presented themselves. Sometimes we came out the other side just glad we had made it.

Safety rules were not high on Chris's priority list, which you needed to take into account when he offered you the "I would" guidance. Almost every story about Chris included his legendary five o'clock vodka OJ and so did his escapades.

First of all, no one in the history of man before or after Chris Connors has called it a "vodka OJ." It's called a screwdriver. We have no idea why Chris persisted with "vodka OJ" as the moniker, but it is cooler to say if we have to admit it. We still call the drink that now because of him, and even our friends order it that way too.

If you were with him around five o'clock, you'd hear the rattling of ice in his red, plastic, pebbled tumbler with "Enjoy Coca-Cola" on it (the kind you'd find at an outdoor fish n' chips restaurant or in a diner where they serve toast cold). If he saw you nearby, he'd say something like, "Hey, you can join or not join. This is my journey right now. I'm having a vodka OJ," and, of course, you'd inevitably join in.

But for those new Connors-aholics beware: any Connors tends to start early and do the Irish disappearance around 11:00 p.m./11:30 p.m.

His Irish goodbyes were all well and good until we were in the middle of another country with no cell phone and no one knew if he was safe or even within the country's borders. That's where we had to draw the line on Chris's witching-hour disappearances.

This lesson began one Thursday in 2000 when we were at our desks at work. Chris L. was on the phone with him, saying he was going to be on vacation the following week and wouldn't be trading. Chris L. had a 7:00 p.m. flight to Asia to see the Hong Kong Sevens Rugby Tournament for the weekend, and then he'd stay to go to the beautiful beaches the week afterwards. The Hong Kong Sevens is analogous to the Kentucky Derby—mainly just a party with some live sports in the background. On a lark, as was customary for our group of friends at the time, Chris L. told Chris, "You should come." They both laughed. Chris had to be back at work Monday, so it was just an unheeding jest.

Twenty minutes later, Chris called back. He had already booked himself on the Friday afternoon flight. He was not taking off work on Monday. For anyone doing the math at home, that's roughly eighteen hours to fly there, eighteen hours in Hong Kong, and eighteen hours flying home.

Sure as could be, Chris showed up in Hong Kong the next day and fell in line with Chris L.'s imbibing group of friends without missing a beat. Everything was fine until he faded from the party just after midnight, without telling anyone, so he could make his flight back to New York City. The legend of Chris Connors grew another chapter that night as everyone searched the streets of China and used payphones to try and find what we were starting to believe was just a figment of our imaginations (*Did Chris really come to Hong Kong today?*). That experience resulted in one new rule that no one needed explicitly defined but Chris: no Irish goodbyes allowed in other countries.

That Hong Kong weekend was probably the only weekend in Chris's whole life that he didn't spend in Lavallette, New Jersey, at his beach house. His house there was great: not great in the large, fancy, sort of way; not great in the sense you'd imagine from his paycheck. It was just a humble, first-floor rental with carpet, Softsoap liquid hand

soap from the five and dime store, and those pastel water-
colors of dunes and seagulls that no one ever buys but
somehow always adorn seaside homes. He'd drive down
to the Shore on Friday right from work, park the car in his
pebble driveway, then go in the house to put on a bathing
suit and immediately out the back sliding doors to jump in
the ocean.

"You gotta wash the city off of you," he told us. It was
his weekend-starter tradition no matter the season or time
of night.

He never spent a weekend night in the city when we
knew him. Fifty-one out of fifty-two weekends—summer,
winter, fall, spring—he was always down at his Shore house
on New Jersey Avenue.

For those two days of relief, Chris cooked the only
three things he knew how to make: steak on the grill, baked
potatoes, and pasta. He'd go see a matinee movie on both
Saturday and Sunday in the winter and fall, and in the
summer and spring he was in the water and reading on the
beach. At the end of the summer, he'd empty his fridge of
all the Rolling Rock and Bass Ale beer bottles lining the
door, dump them into a big gravy pot, drop in some sliced
Hebrew Nationals, and boil them. Those beer dogs signaled

the end of summer and were the best hot dogs you could eat on a buttered-and-toasted potato bun.

Chris also loved to skinny-dip any chance he had, but he especially loved a good night swim in the sea as unclad as a pinniped. Once when we were with him in Lavallette, we got to see the majestic beast in his natural habitat. Unfortunately, we took our girlfriends at the time who did not know they had tickets for this type of show. Standing on the beach one night looking out to the ocean horizon line, Chris didn't give any of us a warning before peeling off his clothes in the sand and taking three running strides before diving head-first into a wave, his ass as white as the moon that illuminated it.

It was during the end of Chris's crazy New York City days that our time as his cast members was called to an end. We'd spent many nights with him but hardly ever saw him past midnight; then eventually we all saw him less and less on weekends. As the first decade of the 2000s came to a close, he was more likely to be in Bar Harbor, Maine, the light at the end of his tunnel, than at Wollensky Grill, a city steakhouse staple surrounded by the buzz of taxis and money.

That house in Maine was his dream home. Chris always told us that he imagined himself buying a big house one day. When you grow up in Massachusetts, the definition of success was having a house in Cape Cod. So the first time he got a bonus check, more money than he'd ever seen in his life, he drove out to Cape Cod where he quickly discovered he was not that rich. So he got back in his car, a blue Saab convertible, and kept driving north. He noticed something interesting happening: the farther he drove north, the prettier and prettier it got and the cheaper and cheaper houses were.

"I could see where these two lines were going," he explained to us. "At some point, there's going to be a connection."

That connection of beauty and affordability was a piece of land on the coast of Bar Harbor at the foot of Acadia National Park. He bought it immediately and, paycheck by paycheck, he built it, writing checks for lumber, then windows, then appliances. The closets were all cedar, and the view out the windows were all pinetree tops and rocky coast. It was anyone's dream home.

A few months before his retirement, Chris met Emily, a girl who eventually became the light of his life and the mother to his two young boys. Chris met Emily on a Thursday night, and on Friday night he invited her over to play pool at his house on the cliff. We were there that night, and we were instructed that our job was to hang out with Chris's daughter, Caitlin, so that he could make the move that changed the rest of his life for the better. Meeting a family was pretty rare in our business; we dealt with a lot of people who had teenage kids, but Caitlin was the only one whom we met. No one else would do that but Chris; he had a way of making us feel like family.

After meeting his future wife on Friday, he continued to create memories with us that weekend. After dinner Saturday night, it came up in conversation that neither of us had ever fired a gun before.

"Oh my God," Chris said. "We have a problem."

He got up suddenly from the table and looked out the windows onto the treeline. He turned to us, looking frightened.

"You're going to have to learn to shoot guns on the fly— the trees are attacking us. You don't see them? The trees ...they're attacking us!"

We were then instructed to go down to his gun room and get a shotgun to defend ourselves from the trees he told us were threatening our safety. We woke up the next day completely bruised and hungover, the treeline no worse for the wear.

When Chris retired a few years later, he flew us up to Bar Harbor for a celebration trip. No wives. No girlfriends. Just us playing cards with his new best friends, Butch and Bob, a lobsterman in overalls and the local bakery store owner, respectively. We had been replaced; these were Chris's new friends and the Thirsty Whale Tavern was his new watering hole. This was Chris's new life, a quilt he had created by stitching a few inches during every weekend stay (he left Wall Street on Friday afternoons and many times drove back down to the city Monday morning to be at the desk by the opening bell).

Years later, Chris sold the Bar Harbor house to some Red Hat guy moments before the tech crash. After the sale went through, he started to overthink, getting nervous he had made a mistake selling his Maine sanctuary. To help his anxiety, he bought a bigger house four hours south in York, Maine, before the sale money had even hit his bank account.

After Chris fell in love with Emily he stopped renting the beach house and started spending more time in the house he built in Bar Harbor and then in York, Maine, after that. His retirement wasn't the case of a fading star; his legend wasn't archived—it simmered into something more mature but just as spirited.

Our suspicions that Chris wasn't about to recede into early dinners and armchair nostalgia were confirmed when he bought a Ribcraft, one of those inflatable high-speed boats made for first responders and the military. Most retirees found themselves on a Boston Whaler or Pershing eating shrimp cocktail, but Chris bought a boat you needed a helmet and a chiropractic appointment just to ride. He was obsessed with the Navy SEALs (who happened to use Ribcrafts), eventually finding his way not just into Navy SEAL adventures but also his own water adventures during his Act Two. He donated to the York Fire & Rescue and used his Ribcraft to help their Search and Rescue team save drowning deer and tourists in those choppy coastal waters.

Chris told us he sat in his big living room, staring out his windows that overlooked York Harbor, to keep an eye out for FLOOKs with his radio in hand. He told us FLOOKs were the primary job for water rescue in York Harbor:

fat ladies out of the kayak. During the summer months, tourists would get too far out in their sea kayaks and tip over in the rough waves; that's when his radio crinkled loudly over the sound of someone saying, "FLOOK!"

Chris was in the water constantly, whether it was the ocean for Search and Rescue or in his pool at home overlooking the York river. He played Boz Scaggs and Al Green on his outdoor speakers as he skinny-dipped in the pool he kept as chilled as the ocean. (This once-charming display of living life to its fullest oxidized to indecorous in the eyes of local parents once his young sons grew old enough to invite their friends over.)

Whenever he wasn't in the water, Chris's garage in York housed various trinkets that he used for his new hobbies. There were two, giant, wooden boxes stacked in the back of the garage, behind his framed Golden Gloves photo and teak patio chairs. In these boxes were taxidermy animals: a bear he shot in western Russia and a lion he had shot on safari, neither of which Emily wanted in the living room of their family home. To be fair, Emily supported, if not copiloted, many memorable nights, but the open-mouthed, dead-eyed lion staring at her at breakfast was where she drew the understandable line.

Selfishly, it was hard on us when Chris left Manhattan to start his other life—hard because he never wanted to come back to the city. He left because he was getting older and because 9/11 greased the skids of aging. He was going to bed earlier and going out less. Falling in love with a nice girl will do that to a man.

Chris had done everything professionally he wanted to do: he had saved enough money, he had met the perfect girl, and he wanted to live in Maine. He was ready to move on and it made complete sense. The part that was sad was that he never came back; he didn't like being in the city anymore. He was uncomfortable in New York City once he realized he had watched all the channels available to him. And once he realized there was nothing new to see, his eyes looked upward toward the horizon.

Chris was one of the few people who taught us that you don't have to pack it in early at the end of your life. If you stay in shape, enjoy your family and friends, and keep trying new things, then the slow-down age gets pushed back by twenty years. Chris ran the Boston Marathon with us in his fifties (and beat our time). Chris went mountain biking in Moab, Utah, for three days when he was sixty years old. We admired Chris because he was great at looking forward like that, at keeping moving and staying living.

Chris also taught us about dying. He had begun thinking about it when he first met Emily, and then more over the last year of his life. When we came to visit him that last year, he was half the weight (no burgers) and half the color (no tan) than when we last saw him. He said he was content; he had done so many things in his life and knew he was lucky for having done so much.

We talked about everything that last weekend we were with him, and we held together our emotions until we were in the driveway about to head back on I-95 South to the big city. He was standing on the porch of his house when we turned to say goodbye to him from our car.

"See you in Heaven," he said as he waved. It was the last time we saw him.

[Chris L. lives in New York with his wife and three daughters. Neeraj B. lives in lower Manhattan with his two sons.]

Chapter 5

STAY WITH ME

December 2013. York, Maine

On a December day three years before my dad's final winter, I drove the eight hours to stay with him for my Christmas vacation, as I did every year. It was midnight in the Maine woods and the only sound was the gravel under the tires of my Volkswagen Beetle as I summited Rams Head Lane. In the daylight you could see that the long, unpaved road was surrounded by rocky hills on one side and open farmland on the other. Only three houses lined the long road, and as you approached his home a miniature white fence came into view, outlining a field of wildflowers in the spring and a field of snow in the winter. A miniature bridge peeked out from its elevated stand above a small brook in the middle of his acreage. The trees graduated from wild forest congestion to perfectly sparse landscaping; the open space between each now-shorn trunk mathematically calculated to look like you were viewing a futuristic AI-interpretation of what a "forest" should look like.

This visually satisfying vista was illuminated in all the right areas by upward-facing lights. It was an OCD-owner's paradise, a perfect balance of light and dark, of nature and space, of peace and well-planned action.

The windows on my dad's home always emitted a warm interior light. In the winter the shadows in those windows moved as life rushed about and, in the summer, the people who owned those shadows emerged to splash and laugh outside by the pool. As I drove up to the house in the total arctic darkness, I could see everyone in the house move from room to room as they laughed or tipped up a glass. I thought this is what it must be like for the newly dead looking in on the people you love from somewhere beyond—like walking on a pitch black street at night, passing windows into houses and seeing life, but life not seeing you.

I was always nervous before entering Dad's house for the first time. My Volkswagen Beetle was fueled by dreams and usually the last twenty-dollars or so I had in my bank account, just enough to keep the fuel gauge hoovering at an acute angle, a purgatory of anxiety. I knew my dad started off happy to see me, and then by the second day, he more or less retreated into his own mind or into his office to plan his next trip with his SEAL friends. I also knew that the longer I stayed at his house, the higher the probability I would make a mistake like forgetting to walk the dogs and then my hard-earned stock would crash again. It seemed like for the past few years his patience had grown thin with me; my decisions (small or large) seemed to grate on him.

My dad's house was always full of guests, friends either staying the night or just magnetized to the energy and love that Emily and Dad emitted together. This house was the North Star to more people than just me. Everyone wanted to be in their company; my jealous mind reminded me that it was never just the family together, and so my few visiting days had to be shared with other guests.

I no longer let my mind stay homesick for a feeling that wasn't guaranteed in my future: time alone together. I had broken through that permanent waiting room of nostalgia to a forced place of living in the present, which meant that quality time was turning into whatever time I had with them, no matter who was around.

Longing to connect with my dad in his new life, I tried not to think back to when I had him all to myself on weekends. In contrast to my fixations, my dad and Emily moved through life seemingly without a thought of the past; they were too busy writing their own endings. Anyone who wanted to be a part of that horizon had to throw their baggage overboard in order to climb in. For them, life unfolded. For me, life was a labyrinth where each turn took an effort of mind and body, a constant balance of pros and cons before the decision was made—a turn in a maze that never ended at the lazy river of life I kept seeing other people enjoy.

I pulled up to the cul-de-sac and turned right between the two stone columns of our driveway. Each craggy column had a glass lantern on top that filled with bugs in the summer, a chore Dad enjoyed taking care of because it was a way to maintain his piece of paradise in a world that had always threatened him with things he couldn't control.

I parked near the garage next to cars I didn't recognize; my heart pounding in excitement that maybe this time I'd do everything right in his eyes. I was suddenly the new kid at school invited to my first party, hoping and praying that being myself was enough to be accepted, instead of having to constantly try to remember the steps of a dance that didn't come naturally. Maybe tonight no one would notice that this wasn't my first language, the language of happiness and ease and fortune. In a life where I kept taking the hits, I was struggling to speak with a tongue that wasn't always tied up with propitiation.

I turned off the Beetle and looked in the back seat at my dog Bambi, a miniature Shiba Inu the color of pumpkin and of cream. She had been sleeping quietly on a blanket in the back for eight hours, a poised, confident beast that was gentle and polite and perfectly symmetrical with pointed ears like furry tortilla chips. A dog was exactly what I needed at this time in my mercurial twenties. She offered me the sort of family I didn't realize I was missing, always there on Sunday mornings in bed, there for long car trips I used to take alone, there when the whole world seemed to be doing something else.

Getting a dog was a decision that no one supported and that reminded me of a time when I was self-assured. That youthful confidence was now a distant memory that I tried to grasp onto, as you do a good dream that you woke from—the longer you are awake, the farther it gets.

I got out of the car and grabbed a J.Crew navy-green, wool peacoat I had found in one of my hunts at T.J. Maxx (treasures like this meant I had beat the system and emerged refined, on a budget that wasn't meant for tailored things). I lifted the front driver's seat to let Bambi out of the car into the cool and clean Maine night air that gave her an instant animalistic jolt. She darted to smell something exciting in the trees while I opened my trunk and lifted out my luggage, a Coach bag Emily had gotten me a few Christmases ago that I was scared to use on flights (what if it got scratched?). I had filled that beautiful luggage with my best outfits and softest sweaters, excited to show that I could dress the part (if the part was still the rules I remembered from last time) of being accomplished in this house of accomplished people.

I called for Bambi, buttoned the last few buttons on the coat (a peacoat always looks best fully buttoned), and threw my luggage over my right shoulder. Bambi padded up next to me, and I grabbed her with my free left arm, hoisting her up on my side, both of us looking hopefully forward. I opened the wide, custom, wooden door to a house of life, sound, and light.

Within seconds of calling, "I'm home!" I was greeted with kisses and hugs from Emily, and I heard Dad yell my name somewhere off in the kitchen, his smiling face emerging before me, as red as the Christmas lights on the tree.

My dad and I seemed to be finally enjoying each other's company this year. I knew he was getting closer to me because even on nights like this, surrounded by people, he'd find a space for a whisper between the two of us in the din of the evening and say, "I have a piece of steak for just us," then reveal some amazing T-bone that was marinating in Lea & Perrins Worcestershire sauce under tin foil on the counter. It was his way of bonding with me, the way we used to bond over food at the diner in Lavallette,

New Jersey, when I'd eat two whole waffles just to impress him so he'd tell his friends about me.

The steaks stayed marinating just as long as the partygoers were soaking themselves in liquor. Then, thirty minutes before he wanted to go to bed, Dad fired up the grill, long past the saturation point of our livers. "Stay with me," he'd repeat to me as I followed him like a hungry puppy to the grill, proud to know my owner had a special treat that made me closer to him than anyone else in the room. When he got excited for something he was working on (carrying the steaks to the grill, docking a boat, carrying a candle to the fuse box in a storm), he simply said, "Stay with me" over and over to whoever looked to him for food, guidance, or hope.

Bambi followed us out to the grill and did her best downward dog, splaying the bell curve of her front paws outward so they looked like a furry maple leaf with five perfect points. Both puppies stood by dad's side, anticipating his attention.

Driving home from Dad's that Sunday was like moving out farther and farther from the sun, or the eye of the hurricane that pulls everything into its perfect center. I was on the long drive on I-90 West through Massachusetts to Saratoga Springs, New York, to a home I had made for a dying relationship. The idea of finally being in a real house with a driveway instead of an apartment in

Philly, especially one near a beautiful bucolic world dotted with pines, made me feel closer to the peace I was seeking. I was about to find out that the more I traced the lines of Dad's life with my own mindless hand, the farther I got. The more I drove away from Rams Head Lane, the closer I got to a home that felt galaxies away from anything I knew, including myself.

I arrived right before 10:00 p.m. and propped up the seat for Bambi to pounce out and make her way to our front door. I walked into a dark house and flicked on a light. Everything was staged perfectly, not only because we were renting the model home of the new development but because, without a job, the only thing I could control was how orderly the house looked. My boyfriend's car was in the garage, but the house was still. It was as if I had stepped into a different dimension, one house full of life and laughter, this one dark and cold.

That feeling of juxtaposed dimensions happened often, that different storylines criss-crossed over my life, making a story I could see only when placing the pieces in front of me at the same time. In this moment, the storyline was a mirror of homecomings, one forced, the other natural. This homecoming was the calm before my own storm, as I was about to be broken up with the minute I entered the bedroom where my boyfriend was waiting to let me know I had hit another dead-end in my maze. He had moved me to New York and now no longer saw a future with me. Despite all my weighing of pros and cons before turning a corner in life, I kept hitting walls, kept hitting the ground, as if I was blindfolded in a world hell-bent on testing my ability to keep going.

There's not much to recall at this moment of being broken up with in a strange city, in a strange state, except the uncharacteristic decision to get into my car and call my father, sharing a fragile moment with him that I normally hid for fear of being chastised for weakness or failure. Right now it felt better to purge myself of holding onto my emotions than it did to be right. I dialed his number and held back my tears so I could tell him what happened.

Sometimes people go through their whole lives without those rock-bottom moments that take the air right out of your lungs, but most of us will face one or two, as is reserved for our species. In retrospect, calling my dad that night was like setting myself up for one of those moments, gasping for oxygen after one of Chris "Spider Spot" Connors's hits. I was about to take a right hook to the face.

I naively hoped my dad would give me advice (come home, screw him, you're better off) like I saw in those sappy movies that made me cry. Instead, as if both men in my life had planned it together, he laid into me with the power of a supernova full of pent-up life, almost thirty years of electricity hidden beneath the surface waiting to erupt. He said I was selfish and spoiled, something he had warned me about as a young gir—something I thought I had mentally fought against in every decision of my adult life. He said I had only thought of myself; I hadn't started a family or led a life to be proud of.

My cell reception in the dark areas around Lake George cut out so there were huge spaces of silence between the racket of anger, but he kept going at me, and I let it happen. The pause in vitriol was a gift: I didn't have to hear or remember the things I could never forget otherwise. I listened as his voice cut in and out, confused because I thought my dad and I had gotten so close to a calm and loving relationship.

Suddenly, he stopped. He was again controlled, satiated, and spoke no final words of regret. I felt I was a victim of someone else's crime, being framed for something I had no part in, perhaps a character my dad had, over the years, invented for himself using only the small interactions we had when I was thirteen. He had, without my knowing, created a judgment of who I was from puzzle pieces strewn about during various biweekly visits or short phone calls from my life in Philly ("I lost my job," "I took up tennis," "I bought a TV"). I didn't feel hurt by his current catharsis of judgments, which is surprising given my reverence of him, so when I thought of the only question that entered my shut-down mind, I spoke for this stranger who was on the chopping block.

"Why do you think I'm spoiled?" I said, not a quiver in my voice. I was finally released from a world of taking things personally, realizing that he never knew who I was to begin with.

"You show up at the house, standing there in your fancy jacket, holding your miniature dog, acting like a princess," he said, reminding me of the exact moment I had walked in his house, Dad's two French bulldogs jumping out to play with Bambi, and Emily embracing me with love. Once again it was the same scene in the movie for each of us, but seen from different perspectives, different dimensions: me striving to look the part to make him proud (he always commented on put-together women, classy ladies he would have never cheated on when he was young), and him looking out from his own universe onto a daughter who had eaten waffles for gifts, grown up to date men instead of raise a family, and appeared on his doorstep with a pure-bred dog and a wool peacoat.

That was the same doorstep that, in a mirrored storyline three years later, I stood on wearing an old T-shirt, opening the door for my brothers after a trip to the mall to help them forget that their dad was dying. I greeted their dogs and yelled to Emily we were all home. Dad came out of his bedroom, more frail this morning but with the purest form of a smile, to see me.

"CAITLIN! Want to see a movie this afternoon?" he asked.

We couldn't, of course, because in a few minutes he was too tired to stand, and in a few months, the nurse's prediction would be wrong: Dad didn't die standing up. He died lying down, me next to him with my hand on his ribbed chest, Al Green playing on an anonymous phone, and a border of family standing around every inch of his bed, just like you see in the movies you think are too scripted.

Past the event horizon, in that multidimensional tesseract, you could see both moments at this doorstep happening three years apart and happening simultaneously. You would see him love me, hate me, forget me, and need me all at different times, all at the same time. All in one home in Maine.

Back in the present moment outside of the wormhole, the light from a lone, Lake George streetlamp lit up the inside of my Beetle in a community of empty lots and freshly staked, "For Sale" signs. I heard my dad's voice on the phone, still lecturing me about being spoiled, but I was staring at the ring on my finger. It wasn't an engagement ring but a hand-me-down from a friend, a gift from an ex-boyfriend that she no longer wanted to see: two sterling silver loops, one curving over the other, each with twelve very small diamonds, like two rings of a planet, two shepherd moons.

The ring made me feel fancy, even if it was a gift meant for someone else, and at this moment it pulled me away from a painful reality as I watched it reflecting the streetlight into tiny dots on my steering wheel, like small burning holes. As I twisted my hand slowly, the universe of stars it had expanded and contracted. Most people wouldn't have noticed such a thing, but I was entranced that the smallest movements I made could change a whole world of light.

Chapter 6

CRUISING ALTITUDE

Winter 2016. York, Maine

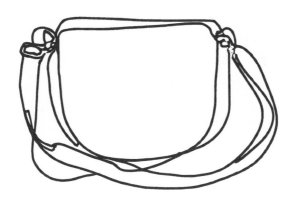

This winter was the last time I was in my dad's home, sur-rounded by his things and his family. During these final months, I slept with Emily in the master bedroom, where I woke with sun and guilt. I was careful to make the bed every morning and stay perfectly still every night because I never felt comfortable "making myself at home," as if I deserved any of this hard-earned sanctuary. The bed had six, big, white pillows atop white sheets and a fluffy white duvet. More oiled ships in storms lined the top portion of the wallpaper walls where the wainscotting had stopped. Rolling over in the bed every morning to the vision of perfectly spaced trees, fresh water, and bright wake-me-up daylight felt wrong for a daughter who hadn't built, earned, or paid for any of it. The aura of a life's hard work was always in everything I saw, and every morning I was thankful to be momentarily in the line of the sun's rays.

Light filled every corner of my dad and Emily's second-floor master bedroom each morning, even on the snowy, gray days that Maine winters were known for. The bedroom was the size of a small apartment, so large that between the foot of the California king bed and the four East-facing windows there was space for a full seating area with couch and chairs.

The couch at the foot of the bed was the perfect place to sit and look outside onto the referee stripes of long pines that stretched up past the roof. You could only see their bare trunks, because last summer Dad had stripped them of most of their branches to have a better view of the York River. Each spindly, white trunk still had its bushy, beautiful green pines at the top, the whole perfectly manicured lot of them swaying in snowstorms, rainstorms, or sometimes just happily still. They seemed to stand proud among their unruly forest neighbors on the border of the property on Rams Head Lane.

The southeast corner of the bedroom had another wall of glass atop a comfy window seat. Most of the morning light available was captured in the room's prism of windows and was made softer after bouncing off the too-high mahogany molding on all the walls in the room.

Dad had bought the 7,436-square-foot home in 2009 after a Wall Street broker, who had built it as his dream retirement home, was forced to sell it. During the sale, the home stood empty, waiting for a new buyer only a year after its construction because of a religious war one continent over that resulted in a big stock loss for the owner.

Dad orchestrated a slew of projects to turn the shell of one man's dream into his own retirement foxhole. The first project was to thin out the forest on his land and strip the pine tree torsos for better views. This was something that the neighbors still have not forgiven him for, but even some admit that it is beautiful to see there is enough space for wildflowers and grass to breathe in the sunlight that could now shine through.

Dad's next project was getting custom wood molding on most of the walls and having wooden bookshelves installed on the rest so that the home resembled the warm, brightwork of the inside of a boat's hull. Ash, teak, cherry, walnut, and mahogany were all inside and outside the house in the form of closets or pool furniture. This particular project manifested itself in the upstairs master bedroom in wainscotting that crept four-fifths of the way up the wall with brown sugar lines, a wall covering that kept all the bright white light from a snowy day stuck in the amber spectrum of the room.

While Dad was healthy, I kept myself at bay from this golden spoon. When I visited him from my small world in Philadelphia, I had a heightened awareness about where I left my water glasses (they could leave a ring of irresponsibility on a custom wood table). The house was easy to get comfortable in, so sometimes I made sure I stayed only a few days, because I knew what my Dad would think if he caught me lying by the pool relaxing in the hard work of someone else. I felt the longer I stayed, the higher the probability my dad would reveal my fatuities. Despite Emily doing her best to make me feel at home, I was nervous to even open the fridge to grab a snack without being able to replenish whatever it was I took, a post-traumatic trigger from baggage heavy enough to give me scoliosis. I struggled just to pay the rent for my Philly apartment, the one whose afternoon light didn't peak through tall pines but instead the iron bars on my windows.

Although I thought I lived a life that erred on the side of privation, my dad wasn't scared to let me know when I seemed to be too spoiled, a cancer he was fighting to kill in his firstborn. His hatred for a spoon-fed offspring was ingrained in him with every stroke of his paintbrush when he painted houses in Quincy in the '70s and trying to figure out how to make a life for himself. He was certainly dealing with the pressure of making his own father proud, a man who said boredom could be cured by digging a ditch.

I was scared to be spoiled too, so I came up with creative ways of penance for my privileged existence—outside of ditches. For instance, I thought proactively paying my dad twenty dollars whenever I used the landline too much would get him to approve of my character. We were both looking to make our fathers proud—an evolutionary domino effect that ended with no game tiles standing.

I had always been proud to be Chris Connors's daughter until that night in 2013 when my world came crashing down and my dad finally let me know what he thought of me. Until then, I was excited for my dad to see how strong and independent I was. Everything I was doing to evince my character to him was, unknown to either of us at the time, just his own blood pumping through me: the stubbornness that fired me up every time I was laid off; the confidence that had me packing my things in boxes after every break-up instead of staying to wallow; and the fight that had me ready to attack whoever thought they could mug me on my late-night walks home in Philly.

Now with my luggage unpacked in his beautiful master bed-room, him sick downstairs, and unable to move because of deteri-orating muscles, I was irrationally scared of him walking in to find me as a stand-in in his life. I was a stunt-double of sorts because in a way I was now Emily's partner: Emily and I took turns being responsible for Dad during the last chapter of his life (or, to us at the time, the holiday season). He was downstairs, away from our view, and we were like new parents taking turns with a baby who could roll over and suffocate themselves in the crib or stick a curious finger in a tempting electrical outlet. Instead of late-night nursery cries, we had late-night drug-induced wanderings.

Dad had requested more pain medicine because he had become dubious of Emily's and my ability to get him what he needed, despite our copious notes and pushover sensibilities. Every day, on a new, 8.5" x 11" colored piece of paper that would have been happier being used as an origami swan, we wrote down the amount of drugs we gave him, at what time, and with notes. The notes sometimes were the key to a puzzle my dad might present us with at anytime. Notes like "sharp pain at 2pm" and "slept most of the day" could help us decipher what he was feeling, needing, or lying about.

At first, Dad was thankful to have us doling out his medicine. We dispersed his doses on the same wet bar we previously (and sometimes still) used for making too-strong drinks. Slowly he began to suspect that we were holding out on him, purposely denying him a pain-free day that seemed just out of his reach. He was sure we weren't giving him as much as we were supposed to, and when we tried to tell him the doctor prescribed these not us, he thought we were just arguing to be right. He was used to a lighthearted, back-and-forth with Emily and any other female guests who tried to control him or tell him what to do; he liked debating, and for a long time he had a hard time letting go of his desire to win.

I had never seen my dad lose a fight, especially those with me during most of my fourteenth, fifteenth, and sixteenth years (even though I knew I was right). I learned how to fight and debate from my dad, but he didn't expect my studies to be practiced on him, nor did he know about teenage hormones and what they can do to a girl. During our games of Scrabble, when he didn't let me use a dictionary, I learned that debating well and negotiating if you were wrong were just as good as being right: if he put down a word and could convince me it was real, then that was worth the points. I learned that being a different kind of smart, having a smart tongue and sharp wit, was worth just as much as being a studied speller. When I presented my first argument for an increased allowance, he was the judge and the jury. I was proud of the castle-takes-rook moves I made, and my dad smiled and laughed when he realized I was going to be a "bullshit artist" just like him.

That's why I was stunned the day I saw him back down from a debate with Emily one night in the kitchen. The verbal tennis match was about the true expiration of leftover food versus money spent on new food.

"You can be right, or you can be happy," he whispered to me.

I remember him smiling, as if he was almost happy to lose, as he watched his precious two-day old General Tso get thrown down the disposal to make room for new groceries. This was something he never did when he lived alone on 55th and Lexington in his studio apartment. Whether it was Chinese takeout (his favorite) or a fancy filet, he never wasted a single restaurant meal, an homage to (or traumatization from?) growing up with five other hungry siblings when there was never enough food for anyone. (Dad's brothers told me more than once how he kept the salt shaker between his legs at meals to make sure he was never without.) I'm not sure whether Dad saw my confused face when he whispered his newfound secret to a happy marriage, something my mom would have appreciated years ago when he didn't give in to the idea that being happy and being right could ever be exclusive.

But now here the three of us were arguing over drugs and Dad had slipped comfortably into the defensive aggression that had kept him so warm in his younger years. The doctor took Emily and me aside later that day to suggest a morphine pump that automatically dispensed a small dosage of morphine at time-delayed increments. This was a perfect solution for my suspicious alpha father who was being forced to ask a woman for help every time he had a pain, only to be confused later when we told him he already had a dose. He never remembered taking the syringe of sweet-smelling fatality despite the stacks of notebook papers on the bar that evidenced otherwise.

The only problem with the morphine pump (despite being a very clear milestone that no one had noticed during our drive on a dead-end road) was that it had to be connected to his stomach like an umbilical cord. It was a small needle pushed into the stomach fat and then taped on in order to relieve him of depending on any other human, something he told us all very clearly he didn't want at the end of his life. He had also previously told us he never wanted to be alive when he had any loss of bodily function. If either of these things were to happen, we were directed to kill him immediately. However, the details of this "kill me if" situation were never discussed, so we continued to keep him alive in spite of the many exit signs he would have been unhappy to know we passed. Dad was very clear he wanted to leave the movie before the credits rolled on his own story.

Our six-foot, 150-pound baby now had an umbilical cord attached to a pump he was now forgetting on dressers, the bed, nightstands, or counters, which meant he was tethered to a weight that constantly was getting pulled out of his stomach. His dragging pump and tubes were like the chains of Jacob Marley, a burden on his freedom that he was not prepared to carry. His ailments were writing checks his body wasn't ready to cash.

As Dad stood looking out the window of his bedroom, his morphine pump on the dresser next to him, something happened. Sometimes Dad's mind emerged from the turbulent murk of drugs and spiritual transitions, and he would enter these momentary pockets of clarity. That's when he saw you, looked right into your eyes, and smiled from recognition. It was in the center of these hurricanes when you could see him realize what a ridiculous mess this all had become. In his lucidity he immediately sensed the encroaching storm around him and cut through the tension with a sharpened sense of humor or lighthearted perspective that the house had been missing for months.

It happened now as Dad turned away from the window and walked to his bed. The cheap, black morphine bag he was forced to pick up when transporting himself around his own house remained on the dresser where he had set it moments earlier, but his memory was not the best. Forgetting his encumbrance, the pain line to his stomach went taut as he got farther away, like the distance lines he used to use while scuba diving.

"Dad!" I warned him, pointing at what was about to fall off the dresser. "Your bag!"

"This?" He paused, looking back. "This…"

He had taken a breath before smiling at me as he finished the sentence. "This is all the bad home loans I sold."

And with that, he picked up his morphine shackle and shuffled into the next room as if it was just another day, disappearing back into the fog of narcotics. I realized then just how much I had missed my friend.

I had a solution for this morphine burden. Thinking perhaps I could win back the affection and approval of an agitated and unhinged mind (which was telling him things like beating the large spider in the corner of his room with a fire poker was a cogent offense), I bought Dad a camouflage-patterned fanny pack. A joke in its own masculine unmasculinity, I thought it could hold the morphine bag so Dad wouldn't forget to bring it with him.

The whole morphine pump setup annoyed my business sense: what a horrible idea to give a patient on morphine the task of remembering a permanent carry-on in this physical world as their mind kept them elsewhere in a place we couldn't see. I had a career in sales and I couldn't imagine a salesman getting a signature on this hospice product. "I know you're seeing your dead college buddy on the ceiling and don't realize you're standing naked in front of your family, but when you decide to move forward, please take this bag with you, okay? Sign here on the dotted line next to your credit card number for the deductible on your insurance. Press hard please; it's cheap carbon." It was another example of how the end of a human life seemed to have been less thought about from both a product-innovation and psychological perspective than any other aspect of this world.

For a while, the camouflaged fanny pack helped the days go along smoother, with less arguing with him about why we were following him around all day, micromanaging his movements.

Somewhere in the world, at this same exact time, Dad's Navy SEAL pal "Maddog" was donning a similar camouflage fanny pack somewhere in Virginia Beach—one that didn't house morphine. Maddog's pack included a switchblade, folds of cash, and his driver's license so that both hands could be free to drink and tussle, or whatever combination the night presented. (Later that year Maddog took Chris's death the hardest, clocking in more tears than anyone, his measured as Tullamore Dew ounces.)

The days became more monotonous as Dad became increasingly sleepy, but the nights were full of short, vivid plays headlined by Chris Connors himself. Emily and I took turns sleeping in the main living room downstairs, just outside Dad's door. There we had shocking intermissions of wakefulness brought on by the sound of a door creak, a medical machine beeping, or just the cold wind whipping against the thick-paned windows all around us— a bitter cold that was trying to reach for Dad through the walls. We were always waiting for him to make an abhorrent nocturnal sound, waiting for a moment when we were needed by a man who never really needed us at all because he actually never once fell.

Evading stumbling his whole life was even more impressive given that most of his time was spent taunting injury and courting risk. One summer I saw Dad lying on one of his teak lounge chairs by the pool in his swimsuit, holding a stun gun. I watched from the kitchen window as he looked at it, contemplating a crazy idea long enough for me to know this man was retired. I saw him check for batteries and then come inside to get the AA he needed. He went back outside and stood on the lawn for a few minutes before putting the stun gun to his neck and turning on the current.

It may have been hours before his headache went away, but he never fell.

Even just weeks before his death, his son Chris Jr. got an electric Razr scooter for his birthday and whipped it up and down the driveway, never thinking he'd have to share it with anyone but his younger brother. When Dad appeared at the door asking for a turn, having been in a medically induced sleep only moments before, we all waited with bated breath to catch his unstable, semi-unconscious body, but it never fell. Dad rode the scooter around the cul-de-sac as we held ourselves back from protecting him, marveling at the man who was willing to call life's bluff over and over.

The waiting-while-living state of being was a curious ether. There was a constant energy inside of us that we couldn't drain by just physical movement; it was as if we were riding out turbulence at a 35,000-foot elevation, our bodies tense as they waited out every bump, every heartbeat, existing in anxiety as one exists in mindlessness. We were always waiting for the drop. That tense feeling in the house was an intangible change in the cadence of our life, like the pause in the middle of a serious conversation as you wait for the waiter to clear each plate off the table.

One particular night when I was sleeping upstairs in the master bedroom, Emily taking the night shift on the couch, I was awakened by the soft sound of socks shuffling on the wood floor. I blinked to see Dad standing over my bed and Emily appearing behind him.

"He wanted to come up here to snuggle in with you," she said, as if talking about an eager puppy. She had probably been helping him up the stairs for the past quarter of an hour.

Dad shuffled over to his fluffy white bed and finally let his whole body fall horizontally in it, his legs still partially off the mattress. Emily helped him under the covers as he made small movements to get situated on his bed, in his room, for a nap like he used to take in the afternoons after retiring. I was still groggy and happy to not move or be awoken by an emergency that required me to stand, so I moved over a bit to give him room and lay on my left side so I could face him. My head was on the pillow next to his, my eyes on him the whole time, curious as to why he was up here or what he was thinking.

Dad's blue eyes were closed, and his breathing seemed calm and shallow. I thought it pompous of myself to think he came to be with me. It is common for people visiting the dying to put importance on very normal things for the sake of giving something we don't understand a meaning that we can hold onto. Most likely he was confused and thought he still slept up here in his master, second-floor bedroom. (I noticed him regressing to old habits like opening the fridge to make a steak, even when he hadn't eaten in weeks, which was really just muscle memories playing out; in a few moments he wouldn't remember why he was standing in front of the fridge in the first place.) Or perhaps he was just trying to control something in his life (this bed was certainly more comfortable than the one downstairs).

Or it could have been a physical test of strength and mind over matter to climb the stairs (like the time he agreed to climb Denali at an age when he should have been at a tropical resort, lifting the flag on his beach chair to signal to the servers he was ready for another drink). Dad was constantly fighting his body and strengthening his mind to accomplish anything, to the point his friends and family learned to never be surprised when they got a phone call that he was going to run the Boston Marathon with no prior marathon history or continuing to hike in the mud with SEAL trainees even though his feet, his SEAL friends later learned, were discovering the soft pain of trench food. His skin might've been melting off into his sock, but he pushed forward, never mentioning to the group any discomfort, perhaps because it was expected of him to complain since he was the oldest.

I didn't know why Dad was lying next to me in his king-size bed that morning as the sun streamed in, as if it was just another afternoon nap and there was nowhere else to be. But he smelled clean like soap and I enjoyed being close to him again, being able to lie peacefully next to the warmth of my father instead of having to stand anxiously above the coldness of a patient.

2007:
TRES AMIGOS

Created from the memories of Rob Brazier,
a retired Navy SEAL officer who became
one of Chris's closest friends
in his last years.

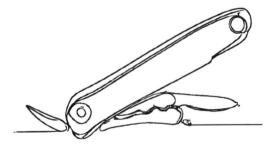

I knew I liked Chris right away when he referenced our Functional Fitness trainer as a character from *Saturday Night Live*, Jacob the Bar Mitzvah Boy. The SEAL workout program at the time was a bit ragged and ineffective, which meant it could be potentially dangerous in the eyes of Special Warfare. This trainer was brought on board to develop a cardio, strength, and flexibility program that was more suitable to our needs and goals. He was now standing in front of us explaining human anatomy and basic exercise science, and Chris was bored.

Chris had previously befriended the trainer and asked him to be his fitness coach for the week, which is how we came to be training next to each other. After listening to the trainer's dry monologuing, Chris burst out in frustration, "They're Navy SEALS for God's sake." I had to explain to Chris that while we all knew how to workout and stay in shape, our methods were a little primitive and we injured ourselves.

When I saw this middle-aged, retired bond salesman standing among the young men of SEAL Team Two, I imagined he was experiencing some sort of midlife crisis, but I could immediately tell he had a strong desire to change one aspect of his life. I saw that he had a Type A personality defined by competitiveness, impatience, and a motivation to achieve results.

Chris survived our weekly workout (for the most part). On the last day, the final box to check was a mountain bike ride through the local state park for sixty or so miles. I lent Chris my mountain bike and sent him on his way into the park with the rest of the team after adjusting the seat slightly for his build. He rode that bike for about four hours and when he came back, he was nothing less than a mess.

Chris earned some new battle scars on that ride, his rendition of tattoos, from various moments of tumbling over the bike. Anyone who has fallen off a bike by pitching to the left or right knows that hurts well enough. But flying over the handlebars opens a lot of doors for new pain and damaged skin. He left and returned with a good attitude, but his coordination on a mountain bike left something to be desired.

Whenever Chris was picking himself up off the trails from minor bumps in the road, a wry expression often followed. When pain showed on his face, you knew a snide remark was coming. He found that something like, "Taking off my sweaty underwear should be considered Resistance Training," could help take the edge off a situation the body would have otherwise controlled. He constantly made us laugh with his self-effacing sense of humor.

"Why am I doing this?" Chris asked during his four-hour bloody bike ride. "Do SEALs really ride mountain bikes?"

He always kept us all laughing and wondering about who he was, which endeared him to the group. After all was said and done, Chris invited Jacob the Bar Mitzvah Boy, myself, and a couple of other SEALs up to his home to meet his wife and newborn son, Chris Jr. That's when my bond with him strengthened; trust was taking hold, a must for any buddy system.

Within a few years, I had half a dozen visits to the north country under my belt to visit Chris and hear about his sea stories or whatever new thing he was challenging himself with (like running in the Boston Marathon for the sixth time). The more time we spent together, the more I watched Chris's character morphing into a Team guy's mentality. He was starting to understand the concept of teamwork, and that started with the concept of a swim buddy, a two-person team that helped many guys understand how putting effort into a strong partnership could be just as important as putting effort into your own success.

He liked the SEAL's mottos such as, "The only easy day was yesterday" and "It pays to be a winner," which were instilled through all our training. The SEAL ethos is intended to inspire, humble, and remind us to strive relentlessly to be better individuals, physically, mentally, emotionally, ethically, professionally, and personally—more so than the day before. "A common man with uncommon desire to succeed" is what is said about us and Chris had that desire. Chris was dedicating himself to learning about our world and was really becoming attached to the way of the warrior, so to speak. He wanted the SEALs' respect and knew that it would come by creating circumstances that challenged him.

However, with Team challenges came rules. Rules that must be enforced, which didn't always fare well with him. (One of the reasons he got kicked out of the Army was his affinity for bucking the system; another reason was that he was told to mow the lawn and instead mowed over all the roses; he was honorably discharged right after). In Special Operations, ambiguity is a constant, rules can be pliable, and exceptions will be made to meet the challenges of a mission. This concept interested him in many ways, and he wanted to be a part of it.

A few years into our friendship Chris called me and, without even a "hello," blurted out, "Let's climb a mountain." We knew Chris was a business-minded Wall Street kind of guy, so we never imagined in our wildest dreams he would pick Denali as his first mountain. Denali happens to be the highest mountain in North America (20,310 feet above sea level), and I suppose the only mountain that fitted Chris's motto of "go big or go home." Who was this crazy Irishman turned Maine-iac whose daily routines consisted of helping with breakfast (Chris Jr. was two years old), reading the news on his computer with reading glasses on the bridge of his nose, and watching the stock market throughout the day? We were slowly learning him, and him learning us, which was sometimes a bumpy journey.

Chris's previous world of finance was one where growth only mattered in investments, not within the self, and anxiety, not calmness, festered in heightened situations. Where he came from, the fluctuations of Wall Street's famous indexes, the Dow Jones and the Nasdaq, taught him that fear and worry were part of the job and those feelings could help you avoid mistakes, the very opposite of what he was now learning with our Teams.

During 2007, the market was doing its thing, but in reality no one really saw the fall that was about to happen the next year. Chris was losing a lot of money (well, watching unrealized losses fluctuate on the screen), had high anxiety about trading, and a few bad years of real estate investments. I tried to reinforce calmness by pointing out that his decisions were already made; there was nothing to do now since the action was already taken.

We were also teaching Chris growth in the face of difficulty, a chance to learn about himself outside of the confines and hustle and bustle of other responsibilities. I knew that training in physicality, mental stability, and sound judgment are a must in climbing mountains, and experience in dangerous situations will continue to reinforce those values. Chris wanted to climb Denali and was about to learn that, just like the SEAL ethos, mountaineering has an inherent code that should be followed: never climb beyond your ability and knowledge. Stubbornness has no place in an environment indifferent to human needs. This idea was a new awakening for Chris.

My SEAL friend Maddog joined us in Chris's expedition dream, and we pressed on by implementing the planning phase. We needed to start hiking and hiking often. The perfect place to do that was right in Chris's backyard, so to speak: one of the highest mountains in the East, Mt. Washington. Some people think hiking up Mt. Washington is a walk in the park—and to some, it may be—but for most, it's quite a challenge not because of the height but because its weather pattern can change quicker than you realize. There have been 161 deaths on Mt. Washington to date, half of Everest, the highest mountain in the world. Three of the most popular ways to die on the mountain are heart attack, hypothermia, and the most obvious, falling.

When mountaineering, you have to take into account the winds. For example, in 1939, Mt. Washington had the highest recorded surface winds on the planet at a speed of 231 miles per hour. I make these points because all this historical news plays a role in your mental attitude when taking on the challenge; all this information sits like the backdrop to a stage your thoughts learn to act on.

Chris loved history and the outdoors; he had read Jon Krakauer, researched the mountains we'd be climbing, and thought he knew what to expect. He was sneaky strong, tough as old boots, and could hide the pain he was experiencing pretty well. In fact, the only way you could tell if he was in pain at all was to look him straight in the face for signs of a grimace or if his speed slowed down a smidgen.

To train for our climb, Chris, Maddog, and I decided to hike Mt. Washington, carrying thirty-five-pound packs that replicated the weight of the necessities we'd be lugging up Denali. The training hike, for the most part, went as planned. But just over halfway up, around the Lions Head area, I noticed one of the telltale signs of a problem: a tick in Chris's gait.

"Chris'o, how are you feeling?" I asked.

"Do you want a list?"

"What the hell," I said to him, frustrated. "Tell me."

"I might be getting a blister on my heel."

"Well, let's take a break and look at your feet."

Chris sat on a rock, unlaced his boots, and low and behold, there was a blister on each heel the size of half dollars, both bleeding into the cotton of his sock.

"Are you kidding me?" I yelled. SEALS were trained to "nip it in the bud" right away so you do not jeopardize the mission, so I was frustrated.

Right away, Maddog chimed in and started singing "Macho Macho Man," which brought on that wry Connors grin. I could tell that Chris knew he had made a dumb call by letting it get this bad, and I could also tell he was going to tough it out to the top and say nothing about it because of his bullheadedness. This was one of the first lessons learned. We reiterated the importance of stopping and addressing any little issues on this hike and especially on Denali.

On that day of hiking and training together, we talked about our lives, our families, and our shortcomings. Above all, Chris spoke about his children; one of his ultimate goals was to make sure they "work hard, have families of their own, have fun, and don't turn out to be pussies."

We trained on three or four more hikes before it was time to get on our flight to Alaska. In those previous months we practiced on a couple of small New Hampshire mountains how to rope ourselves together so we could move as one unit. Chris also conned the York Fire Department Chief into letting us practice some rappelling techniques inside the fire station. This checked the box for crevasse rescue if the occasion should arise during our journey over the glacier that began our ascent on Denali. Once we were comfortable with all of Chris's new knowledge and proficiency in basic mountaineering skills, we decided May 2007 was the best time to tackle this taxing challenge.

Our first high-altitude expedition, more than 20,300 feet, was now in our sights. The excitement was building as the three of us waited for May in the comfort of our sea-level lives. We had the necessary confidence and knowledge to succeed, but we needed Chris to keep that positive mental attitude in his frontal cortex.

On a Monday morning in May, we loaded up our gear in our respective bedrooms and living rooms, left our home-town airports, and flew to meet up in Anchorage, Alaska. We landed and stayed in Anchorage for a few days to acclimate and relax. While going over our gear list to make sure we had everything, Chris jumped up.

"We forgot one thing," he said while turning to the door. We had everything we needed, as far as Maddog and I could see, so we had no clue what Chris was talking about.

"Personalized thermoses!" He said as he left our hotel room without an explanation. In no less than ten minutes, there was a knock on the door. When we opened it there was Chris, holding three, twelve-ounce thermoses filled with his favorite beverage, Absolut vodka and OJ. We toasted and hoped for the only thing we needed now: good luck.

After two days in Anchorage, we rented a car and made the two-hour drive north to Talkeetna, where we took a small plane to the glacier at the foot of Denali. When we arrived, we reported to the Talkeetna Ranger Station for a climber orientation brief, one of the requirements of climbing this mountain. The brief is a thirty-minute lecture on the do's and don'ts and etiquette of climbing. During this briefing, we obtained our mandatory Clean Mountain Can (CMC), a personal toilet created for Denali trekkers that holds almost two gallons of human waste with degradable and removable plastic bags—this was definitely going to be a new experience for our Wall Street "finance bro" who was used to heated bathroom floors. Chris skipped out on this portion of the lecture because he had to use the latrine, as he would say, "right now." This missed CMC lesson later came back to haunt him on the mountain.

Before we could finish check-in, the rangers needed a name for our expedition team. All we could think of at the time, because there were three of us, was the Chevy Chase movie *The Three Amigos*. We recited a few lines from it, and with our Spanglish coming out strong, our official expedition name became "Tres Amigos" (we had an El Guapo to face, after all.)

Now with all the administrative paperwork out of the way, we were ready to be shuttled over to our air taxi, K2 Aviation, to weigh and sort our gear and make last-minute calls or send emails to anyone who cared. Chris called Emily to let her know he was "doing it" and that he loved her and Chris Jr.

Once we were all loaded, we flew the twenty-five-minutes to the base camp on the Kahiltna Glacier. With the May busy season in full swing, the mountain can have 300 to 500 climbers strung out from base camp (at 7,200 feet) to the top at any given time. Looking down out of the plane before landing on the glacier, we could see it was a tent city. Green, orange, and yellow nylon flapped in the wind, dispersed everywhere on the icy ground like sprinkles on a cake. We were amazed at how many people were doing this same challenge—there were maybe fifty to seventy-five tents in a gaggle.

We landed, unloaded, and checked into the Base Camp Headquarters. There we were given our marching orders to find a place to pitch our tent and then prove to one of the climbing guides that we were trained in crevasse rescue (although we had no guide, someone had to be satisfied we were legit before our trek began). Maddog and I harnessed up Chris and lowered him into a nearby crack in the glacier with the guide watching our every move. As you can imagine, Chris had a lot to say while being lowered down the side of a bottomless pit.

"Okay, boys," he shouted from low in the Earth. "I'm making changes in my life, so if you don't hear from me, then you're one of them." The guide laughed out loud, something that didn't always happen on the mountain, but that was Chris—he was that laugh-out-loud type. We passed our test and made our way back to the tent to drink from our personalized thermoses.

After shooting the shit with our tent neighbors, we crawled into our sleeping bags to get a good sleep before our early morning rise. The temperatures dropped down to a little above freezing that night, nothing too extreme. We each had plenty of warm clothes and configured ourselves accordingly for the night chill.

In the morning, Chris got up first and told us he had to do a basic (growler was another one of our manly phrases for it). He unzipped the tent, looked around to a mostly barren landscape, and said in his Boston accent, "We-ah is the toilet?"

"Chris'o," I replied. "It's the green bucket next to your feet." This was part of the lecture he had missed. "It has plastic bags in it. Just take one and go up behind the snow wall and do your business." We were all gringos, not professional alpinists or locals, but Chris was a big-time foreigner at this outdoor bathroom business, especially with all the clothes he had on. We're talking about a man who took three showers a day, laid down fresh white towels for his toothbrush and toothpaste, and couldn't stand dirt or smell.

Twenty minutes must have gone by before we realized there was still no Chris in sight. By this time, other climbing groups had packed up and moved out on the first leg of the trip. I wiggled out of my sleeping bag and opened the flap of the tent; Maddog followed. We both stood outside our tent looking for the crazy Irishman. We turned 180 degrees and couldn't believe what we saw: about seventy-five yards away Chris was completely naked, his bare ass facing directly towards us in the bright sunlight.

"Chris'o," I yelled. "What are you doing?"

He didn't hear me over the wind, which meant we had to watch, flabbergasted, as he did his business on this snowy stage, in front of the climbers walking past, trying to pretend he wasn't there. Turns out he had spent so much time trying to find a tall-enough snow wall for privacy that eventually he couldn't wait any longer and, since he didn't want to get shit on himself or his new cold-weather gear, he simply stripped where he stood. "Wiping your ass with a snowball" became a phrase we'd use for many years about less-than-perfect situations.

Some might say Chris was capricious, impulsive, or unpredictable, but I say he was proactive; he was some-one who got things done. He did it his way, but at least he was doing it, whether shitting on a mountain, climbing a mountain, or buying a mountain. After twelve days and 14,000 feet, we completed the mission Chris had set for himself, which was not the summit of Denali but delivering a friend's ashes to that remote part of the world, at an elevation guaranteed to have a great view for eternity.

Because Maddog and I were part of the Navy, Chris learned and used our slogan whenever he called us with new adventure ideas or to tell us where he was going next: "It's not just a job, it's an adventure." He made taking adventures his post-retirement job and continued to train with us and support the Navy SEAL Foundation. This one man remains the only person who could keep me in stitches with every death-courting endeavor we chased, and I still miss adventures with him.

Chris went on to snowshoe in Russia to hunt black bears (he said he got dropped out of the helicopter like an Irish popsicle being delivered to the grizzlies), to hunt a lion in South Africa (coming back only with African Tick Typhus like a bullet wound on his neck), and to climb into a cave in Utah to kill a mountain lion, not sure if he would ever reemerge (a quicker ending to him than the increasingly labored breathing caused by his recently diagnosed ALS).

I'm sure Chris's wry smile was always present on these quests, and though I wish I could have been his swim buddy for all his life's chapters, that I had the chance to befriend such a crazy and lovable Irishman was my own adventure.

[Rob Brazier is a now-retired Navy SEAL who is still engaged in physical fitness, close personal protection, and mission planning. He lives in Virginia Beach, Virginia with his wife.]

2000–2016:
THREE HOMES
IN MAINE

Created from the memories of Emily Connors,

his wife, soulmate, and partner until the end.

I was waitressing at a cafe in Bar Harbor, Maine, when I first met Chris. He and his brother Russ had come in for lunch, and while I instantly found Chris attractive, I didn't think twice about him. Chris was older than me and was only in town for a little while, or so I had heard through small-town gossip. (Chris later told me he and Russ commented to each other in those early days that they thought my head looked like a light bulb or an acorn because of the way I wore my hair in a bun, high on my head. My nickname was Acorn with him ever since.)

Chris had bought land on the water right outside of town with one of his bonus checks. Once he bought the coastal plot, he then subdivided and sold off parcels to fund the building of his dream home on Mount Desert Island as far away from New York City as possible while still being accessible enough to go back and forth to work.

Whenever Chris was in town, he came into the cafe I worked at every morning after his run around Eagle Lake. I remember he ordered a coffee and Irish Eyes (fitting, really), a traditional eggs Benedict with a slice of tomato between the egg and English muffin. Even after I'd brought him the bill, he lingered.

Chris came back for lunch and a beer later in the

afternoon, an hour before closing. Somehow he always stayed longer than a normal patron, and I wasn't sure if it was to hang out with my boss or to talk to me. I was hoping I was cuter than my boss, aptly named Bar Harbor Bob, a man impressive with a hand of cards but not with aesthetics.

Turns out, I was the cuter one.

When we started talking, I found out Chris had been in some relationships, a short marriage, and he had a few long-term girlfriends. He told me all the women in New York City were wolverines out to get "the full-ride scholarship" or, as he'd say, "hop on the Chrissy Choo Choo." I've never laughed so hard; I had never heard of such a thing or met a man like him. My quick response when I sensed he was getting defensive about gold diggers was always, "You're too old for me, and I don't need your money because I'm young and I can make my own."

That disarmed him enough for him to feel comfortable enough to ask me out. On our first date, we went kayaking with his daughter Caitlin and one of her friends. Chris had set up a kayak tour and we launched from the rocky beach between the town dock and The Bar Harbor Inn. A few of my friends were kayak guides for the summer, so I had been kayaking a bit already and considered myself decent. I knew the basics, but I honestly didn't know if Chris had ever been in a kayak before.

The girls and I were nestled in our kayaks, waiting for Chris to get in his, but the minute he put a foot in the water, I knew he was going to dump it. The correct way to get in a kayak is to straddle it while in the water but still aground a little so that once you're in you can easily use your paddle to push out into the water. All you have to do is sit your butt down, find your center of gravity, and then pop your legs in. Chris waded out to about two feet of water and then tried to get in one leg at a time. If you knew Chris at all, you knew never to tell him what to do, even if it meant life or death. Needless to say, he flipped the kayak and spent the whole, two-hour tour with a wet swamp ass. Caitlin, her friend, and I could not stop laughing. Chris was really trying to impress me, and somehow it worked.

Many years later, Chris finally completed his house on the coast of Bar Harbor and we lived there together as a couple. Many times during the summers the Bar Harbor tour boats conducted a tour of the shoreline. Where Chris's house was, teetering on the rocky coast right up against the battering seas, you could hear the tour boat announcer and the big boat engine as they got closer to the house. Chris always thought it would be funny to go out on his second-floor balcony off of our master bedroom and say *hi* to the tourists. His greeting was to stand out on the balcony facing Europe like a statue, butt-ass naked, not a shred of fabric on him. Eventually the tour boats stopped coming.

In a way, we became adults together, settling down, moving into a home, getting married, and—he'd never have guessed it—even getting two shih tzu lap dogs, Bam Bam and Dr. Woo Woo. We named Woo Woo after one of Chris's best friends and clients, Tony Wang, who he called Dr. Woo. Tony had two fingers missing at the second knuckle, cut off by the Chinese mafia, and he used those nubs conveniently to smoke his cigarettes. We lost the original Dr. Woo to stomach cancer, and so Chris resurrected him as Dr. Woo Woo, the black-and-white shih tzu with a face that looked like it had been hit with a shovel.

Our second home together was on Starboard Lane in York Harbor, Maine, a house whose walls I am thankful cannot talk because every week it was full of laughter, spontaneous gatherings, and waning inhibitions. Chris always said, "Why would friends and family say no to coming to the only free bed n' breakfast with an open bar and a view of the ocean?" He was right; we had more guests than I can count, and we loved every minute of it.

Chris has a very colorful family, so much so that we sometimes just called them all "The Connors," and people understood. One of The Connors' most colorful characters is Chris's cousin, Myles Connor, a Mensa member and the art thief featured in *Time* magazine and in Netflix's documentary *This Is A Robbery: The World's Biggest Art Heist.*

A famous actor who was interested in meeting cousin Myles happened to be best friends with one of Chris's coworkers. We took this as an opportunity to invite everyone to come up to our house for this meeting (party). As it goes, ten people turned into twenty, that turned into thirty, that turned into the whole bar across the street coming to our house when they heard what celebrity was with us.

There was eating, drinking, playing games, pool, swimming, dancing, skinny-dipping on the beach and then skinny-dipping back in the pool. Someone may have streaked through the party wearing a sixty-five-pound brass US Navy Mark V antique diving helmet. I have no clue what time the party ended, but I do know that Chris went to bed sometime during the night, then got back up a few hours later, poured himself another Absolut vodka and orange juice, and kept on going. The conversations were hilarious and the stories were unbelievable but true.

The next morning, the first order of business was getting a large cup of coffee with a side of screaming headache. Second was the debriefing on everyones' perspective of the night and what were the funniest stories. Third was the cleanup, the first go around, anyway.

When you have entertained for as long and as many times as Chris and I had, you know it takes a couple of days to really get the house back, with multiple rounds of spraying and wiping and loads and loads of laundry. For days, we'd find things like a random beer can or red Solo cup on a bookshelf, leftover crackers and cheese in the bathroom (because someone was starving but also had to pee), and the kitchen counter was a forensic dream.

During the cleaning, Chris and I went out by the pool and were picking up empty glasses, towels, and a late-night forgotten dessert tray when we found a few cigarette butts, a pair of women's panties, and a pile of vomit in the grass. Without missing a beat, Chris smiled, laughed, and said, "I wonder what order this all happened in."

Chris and I moved to our third home and our last, a property that was on the York River and had more privacy and acreage for our growing family of boys and dogs. The build was new and 80 percent finished, so purchasing this home allowed us to make it our own and put the finishing touches on it and the property.

Chris loved working in the yard, planting trees, sea roses, and grass. I nicknamed Chris "Johnny Appleseed" because at all times I could look out the windows and see him in the yard throwing grass seed all around, in the morning with a coffee and in the evening with a vodka OJ in a tumbler. Even though Chris hired landscape companies to do yard work for us, he always was out there next to them, doing their work and most importantly running the equipment. He loved skid steers and backhoes. When the workers had to leave the equipment for the night or weekend, Chris's comment to them was always, "Leave the keys."

One of our annual parties at this house was "The Float Down," a reprise of an event that his brother Russ used to host in Kittery. Russ had grown tired of hosting the event, so we asked if we could take it over, moving the tradition from Chauncey Creek in Kittery to the York River. And so, the Connors' York River Float Down was born, an annual event that only had two rules: bring your own float and wear a costume.

The Float Down itinerary included coming to our house to drink and eat lobster rolls, heading to the Route 1 bridge to launch off (some jumped off the bridge as their dramatic entrance), floating down the river with the outgoing tide, drink in hand, and arriving back at our house somewhere on the river bank. You could float on whatever you wanted and we saw it all: tubes, pool toys, kayaks, canoe, SUPs, large eight-person floats, whalers, metal boats, a homemade floating picnic table, a tree log cut just that morning, pirate ships, and a Batmobile. Up until the summer before he passed away, Chris always eschewed a float and swam the river. And even though he couldn't swim during The Float Down that last summer, he jumped off the bridge, suspended in air for a good four seconds before hitting that crisp Maine water.

Since this was a true Connors' event, costumes and cross-dressing were always encouraged. Over the years we floated down with the Jersey Shore cast, Peter Pan, Sharknado, Beverly Hillbillies, Pirates of the Caribbean,

Batman, Batwoman, and Jimmy Buffett. One year, Chris dressed up as the Crocodile in Peter Pan, Tick-Tock. He had a homemade crocodile head and tail made out of foam, and he swam the full event grabbing people's legs in the water. He was going to make a foam crocodile body, but that proved too difficult, so instead he threw on a black contractor's bag and wrote the words "old turd" on it with duct tape. When questioned why the combo of costumes (a crocodile and a turd), he simply replied, "It's my costume. Fuck off."

As the years went on, our Float Down attendees list doubled to almost two hundred people. At that point we hired a lifeguard for our pool and a couple of people to help with food, cleaning, and making drinks. We had reached our entertaining limit, especially when it came to making drinks at the rate people wanted them.

That house on Rams Head Lane was always full of people, like we wanted for all our homes. Even on the day Chris died, his room was full of people who still just wanted to be around him. We all stood around his bed, making it hard for even hospice care to get in or out. When someone broke the silence of the room to announce that his chest had stopped rising and falling, it was as if someone had suddenly turned off the music and turned on the lights at a party. The room felt empty even though we were all there, shoulder to shoulder, looking at a body that used to be his. To continue life felt like being left at a function once your favorite person had left. None of us wanted to be there anymore without Chris.

We sold that house soon after the party had died and moved across the river into a three-bedroom single-family home in a residential neighborhood. I now stand in as both the mom and dad for our two sons, both who were on their way home from school that day Chris died but didn't make it in time to say goodbye.

I still sometimes have people over, and they'll gather around our small kitchen island, but I don't play music like we used to, and my stomach doesn't hurt from laughing as much. And even though Chris pulled that early Irish goodbye he was known for, this time he's not waiting at home for me in my bed anymore.

Can I go back and relive it all again? I'll do the hard stuff too, I promise. Retelling Chris's stories has made me remember that, at one time, I had it all.

[Emily Connors still lives in York, Maine, with her two sons, Chris Jr. and Liam, and has not remarried.]

Reprint of a letter from
Emily Connors to Chris Connors

To My Chris,

I close my eyes and I see you. I dream that you are just away on some crazy trip you've planned: hiking Denali, hunting in Russia, traveling with buddies out West, flying crazy amounts of miles for a minimal time at a destination. When I open my eyes and reality sets in I see everything we had, all our dreams and goals are gone. We were always longing for a simpler life but our time has run out.

You had this amazing presence to be able to take my breath away (in a good way, especially when you wore a suit) and give it back with a renewed sense of life. You are still in every part of my life: daily thoughts, decision making, raising our boys, carrying on your passions in life that became mine through our 20-year relationship; you are a vision in all my dreams. I remember you at your best, not how I last saw you, lying in our first-floor guest bedroom because you could no longer make it up to our bedroom. You were so very sick, sad, 90 pounds, and in a coma. You fought until the end, but you couldn't talk your way out of this one.

If I remember you at your best then your best was that
twinkle in your beautiful blue eyes (you always proclaimed you
were a Paul Newman look alike and asked that he play you in
a movie) and those eyes did make you just a bit vain; I always
would tease you how you never went by a mirror you didn't
like. Your best was your smile that fattened into a smirk and
the way you grabbed for my hand because you knew I loved to
hold yours. I'll remember the way you looked at me, when you
didn't think I noticed, but I did and it meant everything to me.
I loved seeing you sitting in your favorite red chair in the living
room or on the porch with piles of books and those cheap
airport reading glasses strewn all around you. (After you passed
away we found over 40 pairs of those damn magnifying reading
glasses (you had both men's and women's). The local nursing
home was happy to take the gallon-size bag of readers off my
hands. The funny thing is I have officially bought wholesale
packs of these newsstand reading glasses in the last year; I'm
catching up to you.)

Best and worst, I got to see every side of you, to know
your deepest thoughts, goals in life, dislikes (there were many),
and regrets. You finally let me in when you realized you were
capable of being loved no matter your flaws. You used to always
say I could bring the love out in anyone because I loved having
that connection, the feeling of giving and being loved in return.
I remember one day together in Bar Harbor when we had only

been dating for a short time and you had thought you were going to be alone forever because of your particularities. I had laid my cheek on the hood of my Volkswagen Golf car (named Clyde after a Friendly's waiter I once had) and stretched out my arms over the car's metal front and said "I love this car!" That's when you looked at me and said, "Well, if you can love metal that way, maybe I have a chance to be loved after all." Up until you passed away I can say that I loved you, was in love with you, and liked you. I wanted to be with you forever. It wasn't always easy and I may have not liked you on certain days but that is the hard work of a 20-year relationship. To truly be loved by someone is a special feeling, and to love that person back with everything you have is even more special. It's like the grand prize in life. I found my person, even though you were a bit (ha, who is counting) older than me, we were soulmates in every sense of the word.

I came from a sad, loveless childhood, the kind I wouldn't wish on anyone. When I was 9 my mother found out she had meningioma and my childhood from then on was spotlighted by my mom's multiple brain surgeries, radiation, chemotherapy, strokes and grand mal seizures. During one of the first of many hospital stays, my mother declared she was divorcing my father (talk about timing). I think it may have been one of the longest divorces in Maine state history due to my mother's sickness, treatments, and my mom's hatred for my father. Her revenge on him clouded her somewhat already impaired thought process. Having lived through this situation, I have no idea how my mother could not see that financially ruining my father was actually ruining us, her children. Here's the real kicker: my mother got full custody of myself, my brother, and sister, but she couldn't actually take care of us physically, mentally, or financially. As a child I learned to take care of my mom instead of learning what it feels like to be safe and nurtured. My father, a raging alcoholic himself, was in no place to take care of anyone. Eventually my dad lost his business and he couldn't handle the depression that followed, never mind his children. Many times my sister and I would be waiting for my dad to pick us up at school and he would show up hours late. I would call the bar he frequented and, sure enough, he was there instead of in front of our school. Like everything in life, though, you learn from your experiences and I don't blame anyone for any part of my life. My life is mine and I am a firm believer that you are in charge of your own happiness. I knew I wanted a life full of love, fun, and caring about people thanks to the friends of our family, neighbors, and some of my friend's moms who showed me that love. They could see there was no guidance in our lives and they would make small gestures like taking me places and buying me Christmas presents. It meant a lot to me then, and still does to this day. Small gestures can mean the world to someone, child or adult.

I knew I would never let my family have that type of life. I have learned to decompartmentalize so many aspects of my life, including the effect my parents had on me. You and I always joked that you can only blame other people for so long, then you have to build a bridge and get over it. When you met me you saw how much I loved loving, and that was my way of writing my own story. And for the first couple of years of our relationship you always would make the comment, "I'm never getting married again" to warn me. I was content just loving you but I also think you loved the challenge. We were married in York Harbor, Maine, in September 2002. You claimed I used reverse psychology on you or you came to realize I was the best thing for you.

I struggle living without you. To still love someone so much after they're gone and to not have them physically is a hard pill to swallow. I cry often and the emotional release frees me momentarily of the heavy load of sadness that seems to sneak up now and then. I've taken a hard look at what life has handed me and decided that this is now my Act Two.

I do have stories to tell about you, but some will never come out; they are ours to keep in my heart. Others I want to share because I want our sons to know what an amazingly kind and funny person you were. My biggest heartbreak in life is that they won't get to know you like they should have. The hole in my heart gets even bigger when I think of these two boys that have been robbed of one of the best people I have ever known. I talk about you all the time and try to keep you present and in their lives every day; I hope my stories help them do the same.

You always said to me that if something happens to you, you want me to be happy again and that I should probably marry Apollo Creed. I've decided I'm never getting married again. I think we did it right together. I don't need or want another marriage for comparison. As unlucky as my life has been in the past, I had luck finding you and becoming a family with Caitlin and the boys. I'm not religious but I thank God every day for giving me the family (as crazy as the Connors are) that I never had.

Thank you for releasing me to keep living, even though it is without you.

I will always love you.

~Acorn

Chapter 7

ANGEL OF MUSIC

December 2016. York, Maine

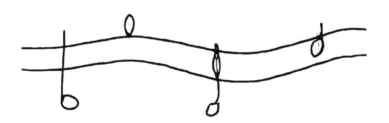

Christmas this year was without Dad, so it existed only for Liam and Chris Jr., an attempt to keep their unscathed but pliable children's dinghies balanced and safe despite the dark seas beneath them. Emily and I had bigger boats to man, heavier ones with masts and gashes in the hull from flotsam, but still lacquered with shine and optimistic about the voyage ahead.

Buying gifts for each other this holiday seemed superficial, tiring, and superfluous—what Emily needed I couldn't very well buy her—so I opted for a sound machine. It was a simple white box that held inside it streams, rainforests, birds, thunder, oceans, and, eerily, a heartbeat. Before Chris Jr. decided he needed the sound machine to fall asleep amidst a flurry of worries that hung over his bed (the poor kid had developed Dad's custom DNA cocktail of anxiety coupled with OCD), Emily and I spent a few nights listening to the sounds of the boxed ocean.

As we listened to the sound machine, in a house without Dad in it, I fell into a narcotic nostalgia for Lavallette, New Jersey, Dad's well-known weekend panacea. As I lay there trying to keep my mind away from the void he left, I remembered the details of our beach house moments, the last time I was truly alone with him.

He had specific decompression methods when he arrived at the beach house on Friday night: he played *The Bodyguard* soundtrack start to finish, cracked open a green bottle of Rolling Rock and made ground beef with brown-sugar-covered carrots. That Friday night process was a beaten path I was glad to join him on as I took a break from elbowing my way through my own forest.

For our Saturday dinners, instead of canned ravioli we got baked ziti and chicken parmesan (as Dad embarrassingly pronounced *parma-jean-ean*) to-go in those round, foil, takeout pans whose foil-laminated lids were perfectly under-engineered to leak the right amount of oily sauce onto hands and glass refrigerator shelves. He swam once a weekend in the ocean, January or August, a tradition he took with him whenever he went. We lounged on plastic, wicker-weaved living room furniture with faded cushions, fabric soft from years of breathing in the sea. We kicked up our feet on glass tables dotted with decor sculptures of seagulls made from tiny little seashells, their points making it hard to touch and to look at. All the ship paintings in his Lavallette house were printed with the same palette as the rest of the interior: soft smokey pinks, grayish blues, sandy beige, and dune browns. The art were boring scenes of windless sails and passive Marram grass in a misty dusk that was lit by the soft hint of an afternoon sun, a silver oyster fading behind a veil of cloudy gray.

On the weekend drive down the Garden State, we listened to whatever new movie soundtrack we had bought the last time we went to the theater together. I imagined Thomas Newman conducting an orchestra for the background music of our own life, scenes of us driving, eating breakfast together, and other montage-worthy moments like he did for the score of *Fried Green Tomatoes*. Just like our Friday-night *The Bodyguard* score, whenever we drove the eight hours up to Bar Harbor, Maine, we played the James Taylor box set. I learned to associate moments with songs or artists and vice versa, and I learned music could control your mood, which is why Dad always controlled his Sonos remote, making sure he was the conductor of the party's energy with Harold Melvin & The Blue Notes. Since Dad didn't talk to me a lot, I also found myself listening to every word of the lyrics, and it was within the lyrics I learned most of the advice that got me through my twenties. He taught me music and music taught me life.

Because of the music he played every weekend and on every road trip, I entered high school with the musical taste of a dentist office DJ: Boz Scaggs, James Taylor, Louis Armstrong, Gordon Lightfoot, Sade, and Kenny Loggins. Whenever I was going through a major life change, my mind silenced the thoughts and dropped an old record from the jukebox of my mind; music became a pacifier for emergency situations. Michael McDonald, Don Henley, Jon Secada—everything I know about love I learned from these songs, from Sting and from George Harrison. They all taught me about losing love before I even found it.

Every night at the beach house Dad didn't use a sound machine to go to sleep but instead played the *Phantom of the Opera* soundtrack in its entirety and on Broadway-level volumes so that the waves crashing outside my window disappeared under the too-loud croons of Michael Crawford lulling me to sleep with the words and moans of a character destined for unrequited love. I listened so intently, knowing my Dad was in his bedroom lying on his back, thick into the deep thoughts the music awakened in him. I could feel his loneliness rooms away the way a dog can sense danger. By the time Sarah Brightman sang Christine's enchanting audition into the Phantom's heart, I was under its spell too, taking on all that I didn't understand around me and hoping it would all sort itself out later.

Remember me, once in a while
Please, promise me you'll try

Music also taught me the end of life; we both knew his life was changing irrevocably when Dad stopped buying music altogether. It was customary for us to break months of our stubborn silences after a father-daughter fight by emailing the other a song we heard that we thought the other would like. The message of the email simply said, "You should download this," and with the link to a cover of "Until You Come Back To Me" that's how we knew we weren't fighting anymore. For the most part, music seemed to narrow the spaces between us as we grew up together, bringing us closer in the final chapters of the book we were unknowingly writing. But our first real fight was also because of music.

More specifically, it was because of Toni Braxton.

As a fourteen-year-old there were very few things I thought I could do to earn a place on the center stage of my dad's mind. I had him on a constantly out-of-reach pedestal figuratively while he was probably literally moving on an out-of-reach limo or plane somewhere. Whenever I might choose to think of him while stuck at my stationary high school desk within cinderblock walls, he was probably out in the world doing something fantastic, his supergiant life the opposite of my average star. I was worried that the rules of the world I was stuck in constrained me, keeping me so far behind what he was achieving and seeing.

How could I ever expect to have my dad pay attention to me if I couldn't keep up with his life, or even imagine what his life looked like? It was probably a life that was not just close to the sun but was the sun itself for any universe that needed one. As his daughter, I felt like a penumbra, but as a person growing into my own, I was just another orbiter in his gravitational pull. It wasn't until I discovered Toni Braxton that I thought I could bring any benefit to his life.

Since I would have a prepared draft of conversation points that I doled out sparingly through my two days with him at the Shore, I planned my presentation to him. I had to plan my conversations, unfortunately, because on weekends when my hormonal mind was particularly self-deprecating, I couldn't muster up even one effort to connect to him and therefore relegated my thoughts to a space reserved for those opinions that serve no higher purpose than to convince ourselves that we are alone.

On one particular fall day, I was at my best and armed with Toni. The rag top on his blue Saab 900s convertible was down, and the beach was going to be the perfect weather for movies, sweaters, and steak. The gray leather of his Saab was worn down to white in all the places our bodies rested. He had bought the car from his friend Kevin, a Wall Street buddy of his who my mom had warned me about. (Dad never told me too much about Kevin, which I understood given that one time, according to my mom, he had stumbled into my parents' home in Shrewsbury, New Jersey, predawn after a night of drinking, and crawled under an oriental rug in his full suit and tie, farted himself to sleep, and left in the morning to return to work.)

The blue Saab convertible we sat in now was supposed to be a gift from Kevin to some golden lady of Long Branch, who, for one reason or another that I'd never understand, refused the car. Somehow his failed gift ended up in my dad's name until the day I got my license and he passed it down to me.

On this fall day in 1996, I was ready to see my dad after two weeks of missing him. I had my conversation points and a surprise: I had just discovered Toni Braxton's *Secrets,* and I couldn't wait to share it with him. I had waited until this moment when he picked me up to be able to add something positive to his life, a life I thought I could barely unpack if I tried. I told him I had something he'd love and I popped the CD into the player.

"This is pretty good," he said as he picked up the plastic case to judge the cover and scan the back. "I like this."

For the next ten years, the tracks on this CD became the background for the best impromptu dancing that happened post-dinner in the kitchen with whomever happened to be over at the time. It was the kind of happy home dancing that comes with good people and a good buzz.

The fight that started it all was two months after that fall day when I introduced him to Toni on our bimonthly drive. My mom called me from my bedroom one day when I had just finished getting ready to go to the gulag of public high school. She told me my dad was on the line and extended the phone to me, which was strange because he never called this house line (he avoided my mom's current boyfriend at all costs, which meant that the closer I was to my mom, the farther I was from him).

"Guess what?" he asked without stopping to hear an answer. He was ecstatic and energetic, and it was 7:30 a.m.

"I danced with Toni Braxton last night on stage. She pulled me out of the crowd at her concert—out of all the people, she picked me. Blue eyes always get the girls, you know?"

I had to put the pieces of the puzzle together as he threw the stories at me. I knew it was the fifth or so time he'd already told this story. Only later would I treasure that at some point in his night/ morning, he must have been excited at the thought of calling to tell me, his daughter, his great moment as if I was finally one of his friends, a star in his universe.

"Wait, what?" I said, face getting hot with jealous anger (teenage hormones).

"You went to her concert? Last night? When? Why? Wait, why didn't you invite me?" The puzzle my teenage mind had decided to put together was a picture of being left out again. My voice went from curious to sharp, and my dad was crestfallen, his happy energy completely gone.

"I'm sorry, I...I mean it was a work night. I took clients. I didn't know you'd want to go," he said, obviously hurt or maybe sad he had upset me.

"DAD! I was the one to introduce you to Toni Braxton even!"

"No, you didn't," he laughed.

"WHAT? Dad, I introduced you to her," I said, in full puerility. "I was the first one to tell you about her."

He had forgotten. Someone these past two months had mentioned it to him too perhaps, or perhaps he had been so caught up in his own thoughts again he had forgotten I had even been in the car with him on that fall day.

"Oh, I didn't realize. I'm sorry. I didn't mean to upset you. I thought you'd be excited for me. I was excited to call and tell you." When I heard the change in his voice, I realized I had crushed the exact moment I had always dreamt of; a moment when he had chosen to include me in his world. I ruined it. Why would anyone want to feel close to someone who needed them so much?

I remember crying and handing the phone to my mom, mad that I had ruined a moment of friendship but even more upset that no matter how hard I tried to swim close to his boat, I could never seem to get on.

As I grew older, I became smarter, which meant Dad and I started fighting more. We began to see the same moments from different angles. We disagreed on everything. The worst of my stubbornness and debating was through my late high school years, through his courtship and marriage to Emily, until my twenties, the years when I'd make all the worst decisions of my life and come out the other side humble to my fallibility. After all my childhood years of watching him silently and revering him unquestionably, I took my twenties to spin out against him—not to refute him, but to scream out I was equal to him, a person who was just as funny, just as smart, and just as worthy of talking to.

When I approached my thirtieth birthday, I gained confidence in myself as a daughter, a friend, and as a whole person that he was free to choose or not choose as he would any other crew member for his boat. I was a sapiophile through and through, but was no longer controlled by the studying or entertaining of one person. I had fought through my twenties without him by my side, even though I had all along hoped he would save me. I had scrapes and cuts and mistakes and memories, just as I had imagined he had in his twenties. I danced on tables at bars the way I heard he had; I had become the center of attention with a quick joke for anyone who needed a laugh and a quicker Irish goodbye. I rented apartments with galley kitchens like his Lexington studio and worked my way up into a career, writing my own story of grit and fun as he was just finishing the latter chapters of his book.

Despite my growth into a woman, I was never able to break through the straight-jacket of his opinions about me, a jacket woven from his perception of me at thirteen years old and that now persisted as a reality. I imagined he still thought I was eating Belgian waffles for money or complaining that I was bored on weekends when I was forced to climb cabanas. I had grown into a different person but couldn't convince him I was worthy of respect. In a way, his pull still had me; it's like that with powerful people, though: no matter how far you swim away from them, you always feel like the ocean still belongs to them.

Standing before him at age twenty-two, he still saw my every word and every action as immature, especially compared to the maturity of his wife, a woman who could clean and take care of children, something he now admired over comedic agility. I couldn't keep up with his moving target of approval. The move from class clown to nuclear family was a sudden change I was not ready to pivot to in order to follow the abhorrent path to my father's pride, an unattainable mirage in the desert of the first few decades of my life. Eventually he came to realize I no longer carried the emotions and petulance of a thirteen year old, the person he thought I still was only because it was the last time he really had spent alone time with me.

When he found his way back to me, on his own accord, it was five years before he died. It started with an email about music of course, with a link to a rendition of "My Sweet Lord" by Billy Preston, and it ended with him finally enjoying my company, his mind free to be in the present. For both of us, it was as if we were seeing each other in color for the first time, the way Van Gogh began painting in the bright yellow of Arles after leaving the mines of Belgium.

I had five years of my dad telling me how proud he was of who I had become. Five years of him calling me (*him* calling *me!*) to ask me to come up and visit. Five years of him waiting at the door when I arrived after the eight-hour drive to Maine, usually at midnight or later; he stayed up just to welcome me home and did so every visit until he couldn't physically make it to the door anymore. It was five years of me catching him during one of his many house parties staring at me and smiling through the crowd of people around him. Five years of me being part of his family, part of his life, for the first time since I had met him.

Lying in Dad's bed in his dream home in Maine, I now remembered the important details. Dad's best and gilded final chapters weren't wild ones; they were the ones the wild days had paid for: a settled life among dogs and groceries. In these chapters he was finally relaxed, happy to watch his oldest son play football, and I was happy he had finally found the peace I always felt eluded him when I was growing up. Both of us had gotten the recalcitrance out of our systems, my destiny fulfilled in his life that I was forced to relive a reenactment to get closer to him or perhaps to get closer to my own peaceful chapters.

The house was still, no hum of medical machines downstairs, no shuffling of feet. Under the impressive paintings and rich wood ceilings of Dad's master bedroom, I could press a button to fall asleep to the sounds of electronic waves crashing somewhere that doesn't exist. Instead of those waves, I opted for nothing. Silence did have a sound: it was dull static, a distant electricity that sat heavy in my ears.

I was now free to sleep through the night without having to wake suddenly to check a morphine pump beep or the sound of the downstairs shower running. As I lay in his bed in the days after he left us, I imagined I was again in that pastel-saturated beach rental, sand permanently in the carpet and the smell of brown sugar caramelizing on the stove. I wanted so badly to be with Dad there, in his hideaway from the mad world he had fought in order to earn his own piece of the sea.

APPENDIX

As per Chris Connors's wishes, he was cremated, his ashes added to the waters off of Great Head in Acadia National Park. He wanted to be remembered for "great head" even after he was gone. Sailors can visit him at the following latitude and longitude: −68.1665937113, 44.3149212322.

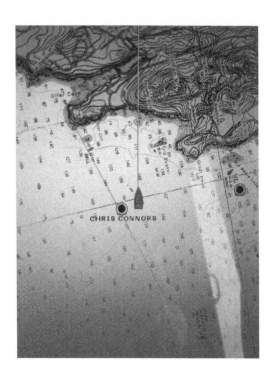

$50,000, 66-Foot Schooner "Firebird" Sunk with $10,000 cash in Cabin.

Quincy police, who interrogated Bill Connors and his wife, Dorothy, of their sons' near tragedy.

"The people at United Brands have been unbelievable," Bill Connors said last night. "They provided my sons and their companions with clothing and medical care, and even arranged transportation for them to return home."

The four young men left Honduras yesterday aboard the United Brands-owned Ronde, a British freighter which is scheduled to arrive at Albany, N.Y., late Sunday night.

"It may have been a foolhardy dream," Bill Connors said, "but most of us had such dreams when we were young and did nothing about them. My sons and their friends didn't succeed in making their dream come true, but at least they tried. They have that satisfaction.

"But thank God for that German freighter. Kevin told me on the phone that it was a miracle they were spotted on the rough sea.

NOW THAT the adventure is over, Connors expects Kevin to return to his job as trader with the Morgan Guarantee Trust Co. in New York.

"I don't know what Chris will do," Connors said. "After he graduated from UMass-Boston two years ago, he worked for the MBTA, but I really don't know his plans.

"Kevin and Chris both like to battle the odds. They knew the odds were against them on their trip around-the-world. That's why none of the four is married. They didn't want to leave any widows behind.

"They lost everything. The insurance on the Firebird was cancelled when the nature of their voyage became known. But they are young enough to start again."

Bill and Dorothy Connors have four other children. They are Mrs. Sheila LeDuc, 27, who is secretary of Daniel Fenn, director of the John F. Kennedy Library, and sons William, 24, Douglas, 21, and Russell, 16.

Next week they will re-live the adventures of the Firebird when Kevin and Christopher come home.

Original newspaper clipping of Firebird sinking

Chris on the Firebird

Chris and Caitlin at the beach house

At his desk on Wall Street

With Mark Zarrilli in Lavallette, New Jersey

Standing with Emily (pregnant with Liam) and Chris Jr.
in front of their home in York, Maine

Before we got the diagnosis, standing as a healthy family
outside the home on Rams Head Lane

Chris (left) in the heart of the house joking with Rudy Boesch, one of the first Navy SEALs and a two-time competitor on the reality competition show Survivor.

In his favorite sleeping position with Chris, Jr.

Doing whatever he wanted however he wanted,
at his home on Rams Head Lane

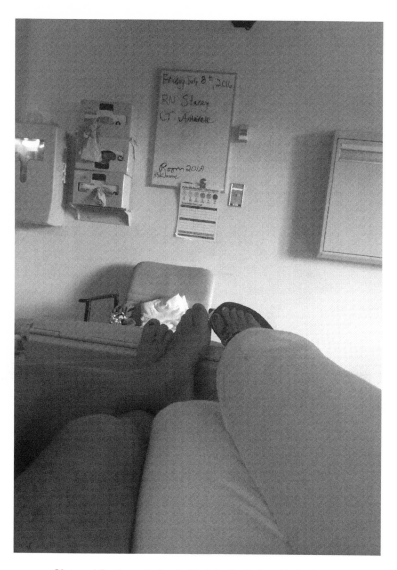

Chris and Emily on the hospital bed the day he found he had cancer.
"He was so scared."

USED CARS · LAND · WHISKEY · MANURE · NAILS
FLY SWATTERS · RACING FORMS · BONGOS
DRY HOLES · SPORT CARS
WIND MACHINES BOUGHT OR SOLD

CHRISTOPHER C. CONNORS

Man of Action

Wars Fought
Revolutions Started
Vibrators Repaired
Computors Verified
Uprisings Quelled
Chickens Plucked

Women Seduced
Tigers Tamed
Bars Emptied
Orgies Organized
Airplanes Driven
Witnesses Rehearsed

NEW YORK - THE WORLD

A business card Chris Connors created and used in the '80s

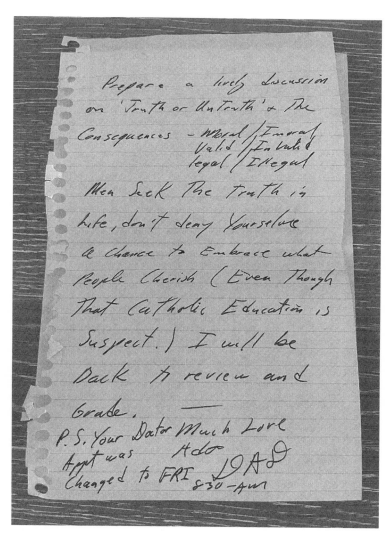

Part of a letter Chris Connors left to his daughter, Caitlin